Teaching the At-Risk Teenage Brain

Sheryl Feinstein

Rowman & Littlefield Education
Lanham, Maryland • Toronto • Plymouth, UK
2007

Published in the United States of America
by Rowman & Littlefield Education
A Division of Rowman & Littlefield Publishers, Inc.
A wholly owned subsidary of The Rowman & Littlefield Publishing
Group, Inc.
4501 Forbes Boulevard, Suite 200, Lanham, Maryland 20706
www.rowmaneducation.com

Estover Road
Plymouth PL6 7PY
United Kingdom

British Library Cataloguing in Publication Information Available

Library of Congress Cataloging-in-Publication Data

Feinstein, Sheryl.
  Teaching the at-risk teenage brain / Sheryl Feinstein.
      p. cm.
  Includes bibliographical references and index.
  ISBN-13: 978-1-57886-646-5 (hardcover : alk. paper)
  ISBN-13: 978-1-57886-647-2 (pbk. : alk. paper)
  ISBN-10: 1-57886-646-4 (hardcover : alk. paper)
  ISBN-10: 1-57886-647-2 (pbk. : alk. paper)
    1. Teenagers—Education—United States. 2. Adolescent psychology—
United States. 3. Learning. 4. Brain. I. Title.

LB1737.U6F42 2007
373.18'0973—dc22
                                                    2007015232

Dedicated to the boys at Southwestern Youth Services

Contents

Foreword   *Marilee Sprenger*   ix

Acknowledgments   xi

1   The At-Risk Teenage Brain   1
    Under Construction   3
    Overproduction   3
    Pruning   5
    Myelination   6
    Three Other Brain Changes   7
    Identity, Autonomy, and Puberty   9
    At-Risk Teenagers   11

2   Teaching the At-Risk Adolescent   15
    A Sense of Safety and Belonging   16
    Capturing Student Attention   19
    Processing Time   21
    Instructional Strategies   22
    Language Development   28

3   Staying in and Thriving in School   35
    Homework and Study Skills   35
    Pseudostupidity: Making Simple Assignments Complex   39
    Transitioning to Middle School and High School   40
    Dropouts   40

4   An Emotional Commotion   45
    Bad Decision Making   45
    Stress   46

Actions and Consequences   49
Argue and Argue   50
Challenging Authority   51
Impulse Control: Getting Mad   52
Indestructible and Immortal   53
Mood Swings   53
Hypocrisy   54
"No One Has Ever Felt the Way I Do"   55
Moral Development   55
Social Skills Classes   57

5   Emotions Gone Awry   59
Aggression   59
Bullies and Their Victims   61
Aggression and Violent Video Games   63
Reckless Behavior   64
Fighting   66
Emotionally and Behaviorally Disturbed Students   67
Depression   68
Suicide   70

6   The Social Lives of Teens   73
Friends   73
Techno Friendships   76
Peer Pressure   77
Conformity   78
Hangin' and Talkin'   79
Dating, Love, and Breakups   80

7   Getting Physical   83
Puberty   83
Sexuality   85
Gays and Lesbians   87
Transgender   88
Eating Disorders   89
Steroids   90
Sleep   91

8 Meeting Special Challenges   95
    Attention Deficit Hyperactivity Disorder   95
    Abused Teens   98
    Reactive Attachment Disorder   100
    Cutting   102
    Runaways   103
    Poverty   105

9 Addiction: Alcohol, Drugs, and Smoking   107
    The Brain's Role in Addiction   108
    Smoking   110
    The Role of Educators   110

10 One More Chance: Education in Juvenile
    Correctional Facilities   113
    Juvenile Delinquency   113
    Legal Culpability   114
    Curriculum   115
    Oppositional Defiant Disorder and Conduct Disorder   117
    Anger Management Classes   119
    Classroom Management   120
    Conclusion   123

Summary of Chapters   125

Glossary   131

Bibliography   135

Index   145

About the Author   149

Foreword

Imagine the amazement when the neuroscience and education communities discovered that the reason for the ostensibly inexplicable behavior of adolescents was the immaturity of the brain. Add to this the conditions that put a student "at risk," and we have an emotional, illogical creature dealing with problems such as attention deficit disorder, drug addiction, poverty, delinquency, oppositional disorder, and a myriad of other difficulties.

Any educator who takes on the challenges of teaching the so-called normal teenage brain has the opportunity to glean much knowledge from recent research that includes vital information made available from brain-imaging techniques. Looking inside the teenage brain may be a scary thought, but many strategies that can aid in motivation, attention, and retention have been a result of this probe.

Teachers of at-risk teens require a brain-based approach that takes into consideration many issues facing today's adolescents. This book uncovers ways to deal with teens' anger, sex, low achievement, and dangerous environments. Familiarity with eating disorders, sleep deprivation, peer pressure, and depression is imperative for educators to understand their students and to help adapt their teaching styles to create successful learning.

Sheryl Feinstein provides the background, the strategies, and the scenarios that answer many of the questions that arise when dealing with this remarkable, if not somewhat baffling, age group.

If we all think back to our own teenage years, we will surely remember that it was an exciting but scary time of our lives. We will remember most the teachers who understood us when we didn't understand ourselves. *Teaching the At-Risk Teenage Brain* will give you the tools to become the teacher you want to be and the one you wish you had encountered in your own teen years. Both personal and professional experiences and current research make this book a valuable resource for any professional dealing with the teenage brain.

Marilee Sprenger
Professional development consultant and adjunct professor
Aurora University, Aurora, Illinois

Acknowledgments

First and foremost, I would like to thank the faculty and staff at Southwestern Youth Services and, in particular, Don Johnson, Rebecca Dreesen, Carole Naasz, Randy Stoddard, and Carol Svingen, for their ability to persistently see hope and possibilities in the faces of lost boys.

Parenting the Teenage Brain: Understanding a Work in Progress (2007) acted as an impetus for many of the topics included in this book, as well as a few of the passages. The challenge of parenting today's teenagers often mirrors the struggles that educators face in guiding and supporting students. Empathy, partnerships, and cooperation between parents and teachers make the journey a bit smoother for all involved in this meaningful work.

A special thank you to Jennifer Sharp, Susan Jordan, and Karen Miller for providing expertise and guidance throughout this project. My sincere appreciation to Scott, Rachel, and James Feinstein, Christopher Sharp, Merriya Pickner, the Augustana College education majors and faculty, and the Sioux Falls School District's teachers, administrators, and middle school and high school students who provided motivation, inspiration, and grounding in this exploration of the at-risk teenage brain.

CHAPTER 1

The At-Risk Teenage Brain

LOL, Facebook, I-messaging. Think of the teenage brain in terms of virtual Internet space: It tries to make sense of itself and its world; it plugs into search engines that take it to the next great academic opportunity or chilling pitfall. Teens relentlessly surf the net for exciting information and activities trying to make connections to the world around it. Some of the links they follow are to the right stuff; others are not. But every life experience that the teenage brain encounters or concept that it absorbs influences its growth. Neuroscientists now have the technology to make amazing and startling discoveries about this unexplored territory.

Did you know that . . .

- teenagers sculpt the brains that they take into adulthood?
- the brain prunes about 15% of its dendrites and synaptic connections during the teenage years?
- communication and impulse control are refined during adolescence?
- the activities that a teen spends time on and gains experience from are what builds the teenage brain?
- engaging in just one at-risk behavior increases the likelihood of participating in other at-risk behaviors?

The world of at-risk teenagers is confusing, challenging, and at times a scary place to tread. Educators can be patient, laugh, and shed a tear or two, or they can be filled with frustration and resentment as they try to lead a group of reluctant learners. One teacher who after a rewarding day said, "I think I really made a difference today! The students were with me, and they got it," a week later said in exasperation, "If you ask them whether they put forth their best effort, they actually say 'no.' They sit there and do nothing—don't hand in anything. It isn't what I expected."

Throwing your hands in the air and cursing the skies is a viable and even self-healing response, on occasion. But in the long run, students are probably best served by teachers who have an understanding of at-risk adolescents. Knowledge breeds insight and tolerance.

Take the case of Jeff, who was born into a modest-income family and was the third of five children. He had loving and caring parents who were not exceptionally involved in school. Starting in kinder-garten, Jeff fluctuated between class clown (he thrived on kids' laughter) and mini-bully (kids would build with blocks and he would knock them down). As he got older, he showed more and more un-ruly behavior; by age 8, he was suspended for kicking and punching his third-grade teacher. He became the full-blown playground bully; he was big and strong, built for the job. As he hit adolescence, he felt more and more like he didn't belong. He was overweight and the other kids would call him names—names that cut deep. This served to fuel his coping skills, some of which were positive and some which were not.

First and foremost, Jeff wanted to belong and be popular. His main coping strategy was to be funny and creative. If his humor was politi-cally correct, great; if not, that was fine too. He was willing to defy au-thority to be accepted by his peers. He and his friends trashed the lunchroom, did petty destruction to teachers' cars, and he was repeat-edly kicked out of school. His future looked bleak.

The turning point in Jeff's life came with his seventh- and eighth-grade physical education teacher, Mr. McGuire. As Jeff explained, "He took me aside and talked to me, about me, not about school. He cared about me personally. He gave me the attention I was wanting. I could see myself as a teacher and helping other kids."

Although there were a few bumps along life's road in high school and college, things began to slowly but surely turn around for Jeff. He has since had a distinguished career as teacher, principal, superintend-ent, and dean of a college, making a difference in the lives of others, with a particular sensitivity to those who don't fit in. He attributes much of his success to that one caring teacher, Mr. McGuire. The power of one teacher cannot be denied.

UNDER CONSTRUCTION

"Hormones are raging!" This simple phrase seems to explain all the inexplicable, often frustrating, bad-boy and bad-girl behavior of teenagers. Teens are children in adult bodies; puberty is striking; and they are too emotionally immature to handle it. Luckily, in comes the cavalry—neuroscientists from all over the world, dressed in lab coats and equipped with fMRI (functional magnetic resonance imaging) and PET (positron-emission tomography) scans collectively scrutinize the most perplexing of entities, the teenager. Information has begun to pour in, and the pieces of the puzzle begin to fall into place.

Scientists have discovered that teenagers don't act or think like adults, because their brains actually function in a different way. Teenage brains, whether at risk or not, are quite simply a work in progress. This transformation from child to adult is typically a prickly proposition for teens, their teachers, and their families, but the trials and tribulations of adolescence give teenagers a chance to develop and create their brains.

Experience, interaction, and learning new information contribute to three major transformations in the brain during the teenage years: overproduction of dendrites and synaptic connections, pruning of unused connections, and myelination—the process of insulating the remaining neurons and synaptic connections.

OVERPRODUCTION

A teacher, Ms. Cole, described to me her students in a rural community: "Some are super-serious: An A-minus is the end of their lives; they take notes on everything you say. You tell them about dinner last night and that your kid had the flu, and they are taking notes on it [*laughs*]. One student, Katie, comes in every day before we have a test and goes over all her notes with me saying, 'I just want to make sure I get an A.'

"And then there's a big group of students that are just getting by. They even ask you what is the minimum they can do. A lot of times, their parents think it's just as stupid that they are going to school. They had the same teachers that their kids have. They hated Mr. Smith, and so, it's fine with them that their kids do. These students spend their time on Main Street, driving up and down, parking, and smoking cigarettes." Little do these two groups of teenagers know that their life experiences are creating the brains that they will take into adulthood.

The brain is made up of two types of cells: neurons (10% of brain cells) and glia (90% of brain cells). Neurons, with their close link to learning, are of special interest to educators. Every neuron comprises a cell body, dendrites, and an axon. In harmony, dendrites and axons are propelling, generating, and firing information all over the brain.

Dendrites sprout in the brain every time that an individual has a new experience or gathers fresh information. A classroom with a great deal of enrichment and interaction may cultivate as many as a thousand or more dendrites from one neuron. Every neuron has one axon through which to send information. Dendrites receive information from other neurons when they connect with a fellow neuron's axon, thereby creating a synaptic connection. Synaptic connections are created, and learning occurs, when neurons exchange information. Learning how to drive a car, cook a pizza, and balance a checkbook all produce dendrites and therefore build synaptic connections.

Dendrites, synapses, and a network of neurons represent knowledge, which facilitates brain growth. Understanding comes from doing, applying, and practicing. It is a matter of cause (what we do) and effect (brain growth). This can be seen in research that compares the dendrites of high school dropouts to those of college graduates. College graduates have significantly more dendrites because of the increased challenges and enrichment in their lives. Teens have an opportunity to build smarter, more efficient brains. Students who drop out of school or who practice a "just get by" philosophy of life allow that chance to slip away.

One group of neuroscientists began doing fMRIs on a group of 4- to 21-year-olds every 2 years. Much to their surprise, they discovered an overproduction of dendrites and synaptic connections during adolescence. By the end of adolescence, the brain contains more than 100 billion neurons, which create more than 1,000 trillion connections with each other—more than all of the Internet connections in the world. In terms of academics, adolescence is a prime time to tap into a person's potential.

Adolescents acquire knowledge at an unprecedented rate. High school course requirements such as English composition, applied math, and physical science all contribute to the growth of dendrites and the making of synaptic connections throughout the brain. Teens who spend their time reading and doing math at an appropriate academic level strengthen those areas of their brains. However, teens who spend time smoking or playing video games strengthen those areas of their brains and will become very good at smoking and playing video games as adults.

Every part of the brain is benefiting from this overproduction. The temporal and parietal lobes are developing, boosting talented athletes and musicians who are strutting their stuff on the basketball court or in a rock band. The difference in ability between the ninth-grade basketball team just learning its positions and the varsity team that is a contender for the state championship is palpable. Short-term memory is getting its own upgrade, increasing by 30% if thrust into action.

Does this potential for learning with ease and speed mean that teens should spend all their time engaged in formal learning? Probably not. Still, at this critical time in development, the more time that is dedicated to reading, writing, math, music, and sports, the better the brain that is built. And there's the rub. At-risk teens do not put time into academics but instead spend time on activities that are unproductive and even harmful to the brain.

PRUNING

The brain works on the "use it or lose it" system. Information that is frequently used becomes easy to remember; the synaptic connections are nourished with practice and become strong. Information that is not used is considered trivial and is forgotten. Once the overproduction process is completed, the brain begins the process of pruning. The brain actually loses some of its stored data (which is not necessarily a bad thing). With the unimportant information discarded, the brain becomes more efficient. Students may forget the names of all the dinosaurs (facts that fascinated them in first grade) but remember important concepts such as the basic elements of a democracy. Every year, approximately 1% to 2% of the brain is pruned, both in a child or an adult. During adolescence, pruning happens on a massive scale, and about 15% of the synaptic connections are abandoned.

No part of the brain is exempt from pruning; this is a distinct advantage for the knowledgeable teen. A teen with a great deal of knowledge about math will lose 15% of that stored information, although the bulk of it will remain intact. This brain efficient process is good news for the students who concentrate on academics; inconsequential information is discarded, leaving room for speed and accuracy in the connections that remain. Unfortunately, the at-risk students who have not spent significant time gaining information in school will also lose 15% of their synaptic connections and now be left with even less information to set into motion.

MYELINATION

Trent and Jason are two high school sophomores who spent a week in detention. Trent offered this matter-of-fact explanation of how they got there: "We decided to skip school; we just wanted a break. We went to Jackson Park and were having subs when a police officer came by and asked us what we were doing. We told him, 'Nothing.' He asked us our names, and, I don't know why, but I told him I was Seth Green, Dr. Evil's son from *Austin Powers*. The school was really mad about that."

Trent and Jason did not make savvy decisions, but their brains were problem-solving complex schemes (granted, not in a constructive way). This ability to tackle abstract problems can be credited to the last, but not least, process that occurs in the frontal lobes of the teenage brain, that of myelination.

The landscape of the brain is fine-tuned through myelination. Myelin, a fatty substance that insulates neurons, allows for faster and more efficient communication between neurons. The frontal lobes—located in the front of the brain and responsible for abstract thinking, reasoning, regulating emotions and problem solving—are among the last parts to receive myelin (which is why we don't teach physics or calculus until high school). As the frontal lobes mature during adolescence, the quality of thinking increases. Teenagers don't think more so much as they think better. They become capable of understanding symbolism in the book *The Giver* and of appreciating the often-sarcastic humor on programs such as *The Daily Show*. The results of myelination are dramatic, increasing communication within parts of the teenage brain by as much as 100%. Eventually, teens become better able to remember information, reason logically, and problem solve than they were in elementary school.

Adjusting to their new frontal lobe capabilities is not an overnight venture. Forgetfulness, disorganization, and poor decision making are side effects of the transition from a childhood brain to an adult brain. The middle schooler is unfortunately the poster child for these untamed attributes. Organizing backpacks, completing homework, and finishing chores are all done in a haphazard manner, if at all. Teachers should constantly keep the word *tolerance* in mind during this time of adolescence—and practice time management and study skills as appropriate antidotes.

THREE OTHER BRAIN CHANGES

A freshman English teacher taught a girl named Trisha who continually laughed every time she heard a word with a double connotation such as *lay* or *screw*. The teacher, after expending a great deal of patience ignoring the situation, finally said, "Trisha, you're going to have a 15-minute detention if you don't stop laughing at these silly things." Trisha didn't stop laughing and was given 15 minutes of detention. Near tears, she looked at her teacher like a wounded animal and said, "I hate you," and stomped out of the room. The next day, after cooling down, she wrote the teacher a note saying she didn't really hate her. The teacher told me, "I was surprised with her original outburst, and I was touched by her note. Teens are unpredictable beings."

That teacher kept it under control with immature teen behavior, but another teacher had his buttons pushed one too many times and just lost it. A girl in his class was smart-alecky, dripping with attitude, and disrespectful. In an effort to get through to her, he lost control and began yelling. After a minute or two, he regained his composure and stood quietly in front of her desk waiting for a response. She coolly looked at him and said, "Do you need a mint?" Not the right thing to say at that moment. Luckily for the student, the teacher had a sense of humor and was able to laugh at the situation. Overemotional reactions, controlling anger, and polishing communication skills are all bubbling to a peak during adolescence, which leads to other changes occurring in the teenage brain.

Aside from overproduction, pruning, and myelination, three other influences are at work in the teenage brain: dependence on the emotional part of the brain, windows of opportunity, and windows of sensitivity.

Teenagers actually rely on a different part of their brain than do adults when they interpret information. Adults use their frontal lobes, a logical and reflective part of the brain, to deduce meaning. Teenagers use the amygdala, the emotional center of the brain, to interpret that same information. This overemphasis on emotions results in a great deal of misunderstanding and misinterpreting of information.

Reading body and facial language is something that adolescents are in the process of deciphering. No wonder they interpret peers' stares as "They don't like me." Worse still, they interpret a teacher's innocuous question such as "Are you done with your assignment?" as a criticism, to which they respond with the angry and perhaps tearful accusation "You think I'm stupid!"

The teenage brain also represents a window of opportunity, a chance to learn something quickly and with more ease than at any other time of life. People encounter such windows of opportunity throughout their lifespan; some are large windows, and others are dramatically narrow.

For instance, a foreign language is most easily learned before puberty, which makes a strong argument for starting Spanish, French, or Chinese in preschool or elementary school. Severe vision problems must be corrected before the age of 2, or blindness will continue for a lifetime. Babies need to bond with their parents within the first 2 years to be socially and emotionally healthy. Babies who are neglected or abused have attachment disorder issues and are at higher risk of school failure and in engaging in criminal acts (more about this in chapter 8).

These are all times when the brain is particularly sensitive to learning new information.

The windows of opportunity for the teenager include the following: controlling impulses (learning how to curb tempers), developing relationships (finding friends and mates), and expanding communication skills (hence, the attraction to the cell phone). Never will it be easier for them to learn these skills, and never are they more motivated to do so.

Adolescence also shoulders a window of sensitivity. Exposure to certain chemicals during this period of development is more detrimental to brain health than is exposure to them at other times. The big danger for teens is addiction. Never will addiction to alcohol, drugs, or smoking occur more quickly than during the teenage years, when, sadly, teens are also much more resistant to recovery (see chapter 9 for more about addiction).

IDENTITY, AUTONOMY, AND PUBERTY

Josh was from a fine family, with caring parents who were concerned about and involved in his life. Friends and other family members agreed, however, that the parents' biggest fault was that the father was too indulgent and the mother was too authoritarian. In high school, Josh seemed to make bad decision after bad decision. He ran with a bad crowd, got caught drinking, crashed his brand-new expensive car because of his own carelessness, and failed a required English class his last semester of school, which lost him the honor of walking at graduation. Although he played in the school band and ran on the track team and although his parents tried to keep him in line, he nevertheless continually caused them worry and heartache.

In an effort to make a bad situation a bit better, his father used his connections in town to get Josh a job at a local grocery store. Josh's dad had hopes that work would be an incentive for the boy to spend his time in a more productive way and, in the process, get some extra spending cash. Proud of the deal that he brokered, the father dropped in the store about a month later to see how things were going. When he happily asked the manager, "So how's Josh doing today?" the manager dryly said, "We let him go a week ago."

The tasks of making his own decisions, taking responsibility for his actions, and discovering who he was were all struggles for Josh. His parents can want it for him, guide him, and help him, but ultimately he has to find success on his own.

It is during the teen years that a sense of identity is developed. Questions such as "Am I a student? an athlete? a biker?" "Are my friends dropouts or Goth?" "Should I drink or abstain?" "Am I Lutheran or Buddhist?" all lead to the big question of "Who am I?"

By the time that teenagers are 17 or 18 years old, society expects them to define their strengths and weaknesses, determine their interests, and crystallize their values, all in an effort to form an identity. In essence, the adult world expects them to be well on their way to answering the question "Who am I?" This is a lot to require in a short span of time. The search for identity is one of the most important jobs that teenagers have, and they pursue this mission with a vengeance. In this quest adolescents try on different roles, looks, and perspectives searching for the perfect fit. One morning, they come to school a hip-hop dancer and the next, a car freak.

Teenagers are moving away from their families, seeking autonomy and independence at every turn on the track. This is a normal part of growing up. Teenagers want to make their own decisions, solve their own problems, and form their own opinions: "I'm wearing jeans to the school dance," "Everyone has a nose piercing," and "Carey and I are BFF [best friends forever]." They want to choose their own clothes, music, and friends. It's a precarious balancing act, juggling the desire to be distinctive while at the same time conforming to the crowd. Teens need adults who will let them make age-appropriate decisions. Too much freedom will be construed as abandonment, not enough as imprisonment. They want to make choices and question adults' decisions, but they do not want complete freedom.

Teenagers can suddenly grow six inches in six months, become randomly sprinkled with acne, and have budding breasts or hair everywhere. Puberty has struck. The teenager is transforming from the asexual child into the sexual adult. This is evidenced by the dramatic physical changes in the teenage body. Middle schoolers describe it as feeling uncomfortable in their own skins.

AT-RISK TEENAGERS

Understanding when or why an adolescent takes a wrong turn is sometimes hard to determine. Nate was a bright boy from a well-to-do family. His early childhood was stable in many ways. He was loved and was read to, but his mom and dad frequently drank and were not vigilant in monitoring his behavior. Throughout elementary school, middle school, and high school, Nate never fit in with a group for long. He attended five high schools, three of which were expensive private schools, and he was expelled from all of them. He was in the gifted program but couldn't pass classes because he stopped turning in work. He became habitually truant.

Failing in school and having a quasi-dysfunctional family soon led to other at-risk behavior. He got involved with alcohol early; he viewed it as a lifestyle. At the ages of 14 and 15, he and his friends stole cars, drove drunk, and stayed out all night. In trying to understand his self-destructive behavior, he never could give a clear explanation of why he acted the way he did. Soon, he was in trouble with the law, was sentenced to community service (to which he didn't comply), and ended up in the juvenile correctional system.

Nate transitioned from a struggling teenager into a struggling adult. He became a father at 20, had difficulty holding a job, and struggled with drug addiction. His younger sister, however, is a Yale graduate and a well-adjusted young woman. Same parents, different outcomes; no wonder we're left shaking our heads. Sometimes, there's no simple explanation.

A small percentage of teens fall into the category of "at risk." Educators view the term *at risk* as referring to students with a high probability of dropping out of high school, with accompanying risky behaviors of drug use, running away, delinquency, and pregnancy. It is the changing brain that makes these teens even more likely to make unhealthy decisions and engage in risky behavior.

The notion that all teenagers are at risk is seductive and elicits our egalitarian nature. In actuality, it does an injustice to the truly at-risk adolescent. An analogy can be made between the emergency room of a hospital and the at-risk student. Everyone in an emergency room needs assistance. For some, it is a matter of life and death, such as with people having a heart attack or a stroke. Others come in with a relatively minor injury, like stitches for a cut. So it is with teenagers—all are in need of help, but some are methamphetamine addicts, and others are adjusting to mood swings.

Some of the usual explorations that teenagers often make include trying a cigarette ("Do I look cool?"), speeding down I-90 ("I'll never get caught"), and attempting to buy soft pornography. I'm not saying that teachers should approve these activities, but they should realize that there is a big difference between catching a cold and catching AIDS or having difficulty with a math course and dropping out of school.

Danger signs that teens are at risk:

- Isolation from family and friends
- Sudden changes in school work, job performance, or athletic activities
- Drastic mood swings
- Lack of interest in outside school activities
- Family conflict
- Living in a community with high crime and easy availability of alcohol and drugs
- Delinquent friends
- Academic failure
- Change in eating and sleeping habits
- Cutting or hurting themselves

Consider Ben. He was growing up in a dysfunctional home. His father had deserted the family soon after his birth, and his mother had mental health issues. His unstable family life put him at risk for a number of destructive behaviors.

Ben began missing school frequently (truancy is the first sign of dropping out). Consequently, he had to repeat freshman English and social studies. He said of the experience, "It's the worst thing that ever happened in my life." By 10th grade, Ben was drinking and running with a rough crowd. One night, he was drinking and driving, and he rolled his car. He said, "I was just trashed, throwing up everywhere. I'll probably lose my license." One of his peers commented on Ben's accident, "It gives him street cred. Lots of guys see how close they can get to losing their license. Well, I guess now he's lost his." Ben did lose his license and eventually, like many of his good friends, dropped out of school.

Unfortunately, engaging in at-risk behavior usually leads to engaging in other at-risk behaviors. The student that is truant is often also going to abuse drugs, run away, become pregnant or get someone pregnant, and/or attempt suicide. There are two reasons that at-risk behaviors tend to cluster. First, the cause behind the original at-risk behavior leads the teenager to attempt other at-risk behaviors for the same reasons. For instance, a dysfunctional family puts teens at risk for running away and for abusing drugs. Second, the act of engaging in one at-risk behavior tends to trigger the probability of engagement in other at-risk activities. If a student becomes addicted to drugs, he or she has an increased chance of dropping out of school, getting pregnant or getting someone pregnant, or becoming a delinquent.

Factors that put teenagers at risk:

- Lack of bonding to others
- Dysfunctional family
- Poverty
- Generations of at-risk behavior in the family
- School failure
- Lack of enthusiasm for learning and school
- Attachment to delinquent peers
- Neighborhood with high crime and availability of drugs
- Early antisocial behavior

CHAPTER 2

Teaching the At-Risk Adolescent

Teenagers at risk are particularly challenging for teachers. They can be obstinate, argumentative, and downright frustrating. Unlocking the key to keeping them in school and facilitating proficiency in reading, writing, and math is not for the weak of heart. A strong constitution, compassionate spirit, and solid knowledge base make a difference in this meaningful work.

Did you know that . . .

- the brain's primary reason to focus is survival?
- the brain cannot pay attention and process information at the same time?
- instruction with multiple intelligences allows the brain to store and retrieve information in a variety of ways?
- language skills improve and deteriorate during adolescence?

Ms. Atkins was a new teacher at an inner-city high school; she'd recently graduated from college and was eager to start her first professional job. She remembers naively looking around her classroom the first day of school and thinking, "This is a bit intimidating, but I'm ready. I'm well prepared. I have a solid lecture and follow-up activities; it's good stuff." She welcomed her first class, and after a brief icebreaker activity, she launched into her unit on the poetry of Emily Brontë. The student reaction was less than warm; she could almost feel hostility in their apathy. How could this be? She left her first day of teaching feeling rejected and disillusioned.

That night, she called a veteran teacher at the school and set a time to meet the next day—she wasn't going down without a fight. She explained the situation, and the veteran teacher mercifully took her under her wing. Together, they took Ms. Atkins's idea of a poetry unit and gave it a twist that focused on poetry found in rap music. In selecting pieces, they were very conscious and careful to make sure that the vocabulary and content were appropriate for school. Many of Usher's songs and Tupac Shakur's poetry met the criteria. The next week, Ms. Atkins and poetry had a second chance.

Digging deep for that special hook, adapting when you are pretty sure there is nothing left to adapt, tolerating the intolerable, and keeping a sense of humor are prime ingredients in defining an effective teacher. At-risk students need in their teachers all these qualities and more. As one student said, "I like Ms. Atkins. She always helps me if I don't get something, and her class is fun."

Ms. Atkins did a wonderful job of matching course content to student interest, and her time in laying the groundwork for learning benefited everyone. The first order of business with at-risk students does not involve tackling academics; it involves time and effort, both of which are needed for a firm foundation that secures safety and belonging before students engage in learning such subjects as algebra and literature.

A SENSE OF SAFETY AND BELONGING

The brain's primary purpose in paying attention is to ensure survival; it is ever-vigilant to possible threats and danger. Once safety is ensured, the brain can fulfill its secondary purpose: sustaining pleasurable feelings. The teacher in an upper-middle-class school can focus students' attention on encouragement and positive feelings toward academics because these students come to school knowing that they are safe and secure. Unfortunately, students living in inner-city schools and neighborhoods filled with poverty are often using all their brain energy for the purpose of scanning for hazards and peril. Teachers of at-risk students must first ensure a sense of safety and belonging in the classroom before they can proceed to their mission of academics.

Establishing no-weapons rules, appointing school police officers, eliminating graffiti, and monitoring hallways and cafeterias make schools a safe place to learn. A positive rapport between school safety officers and students—as can be seen in comments such as "Officer Kirkland is okay; he's easy to talk to"—further enhances feelings of protective shelter. Routines also create a sense of safety within the classroom. Starting class the same way each day, having a set pattern of when and where things will be, and maintaining a consistent instructional temperament all promote feelings of security.

Once school safety is established, creating a spirit of belonging in the classroom is the teacher's next priority. Middle school students usually define belonging as having friends, participating in class, and receiving good grades. In general, a sense of belonging comes from feeling accepted and respected.

Participation in class and encouraging friendships (in this case, familiarity breeds comfort) can be facilitated by small group work. Teachers may not be able to control the size of their classrooms, but they can control the size of the groups in their classrooms. A constant regimen of small groups or pair work is not necessary, but it is an important part of creating a sense of belonging in the classroom, and the results of research conducted by Robert Marzano (see bibliography) on its benefits to academic progress are too strong to ignore.

Small groups need to be structured and coordinated carefully, however. Consider this example of ineffective group use: Nikki missed 3 weeks of school when she had mononucleosis. When she got back, she was put into a small group for a social studies presentation on the Civil War Reconstruction period, but she quickly became frustrated with her teammates. "I was put in charge of the group because they thought I was smart. But I was only attending school part-time because I was still getting over mono, and so a couple of them were mad at me for not being there to lead the group.

"The group couldn't work after school because two of the boys were in a halfway house and had to go directly there after their last class. The other two students in my group didn't speak English—I had them hold posters through most of the presentation. We got an A. The next time we were put into groups, the guys wanted me in their group. I said, 'Oh no, once was enough.'"

There are a number of proactive things that teachers can do to make group work sail smoother. Group and individual accountability, along with class time to complete the assignment, are easily implemented strategies. To increase the probability that small group work will be used to its potential, directly teaching social skills benefits many at-risk students (see chapter 4 for more information). Teens' knowing how to interact with peers, manage emotions, and take responsibility for their schoolwork and behavior will increase the likelihood that collaboration and cooperation dominate the interactions among one another.

Extracurricular activities are also effective. Being part of a team and feeling responsible to peers, a coach, and school staff greatly add to feelings of belonging. Once teens see school as a refuge, teachers can focus on making academics interesting and pleasurable.

Strategies to create a sense of belonging:

- Learn students' names.
- Greet students in class and in the hallways—a friendly smile and "Hi" mean everything.
- Connect new students to experienced students to help them navigate the school for the first 2 or 3 days.
- Let all students participate in making the class rules. (Some school policies may be inflexible, but there is usually some wiggle room in each classroom.)
- Let students help each other with assignments when appropriate.
- Organize your class into a supportive team for school fund-raisers.
- Encourage study groups outside of class.
- Use inclusive words and phrases, such as "our room" and "all of us working together."
- Recognize good work.
- Play an icebreaker game at the beginning of the semester or year.
- Ask for students' opinions.

CAPTURING STUDENT ATTENTION

"He roller-skated into class," said one student.

"She made water disappear," said another.

"He told about the day he got detention," said another.

Capturing student attention is the first step in learning, but there are a myriad of things vying for it. Cute classmates, sounds in the hallway, and the bug on the teacher's shoulder can all seem more interesting than the academic tasks of the day.

The three best brain-compatible ways to attract and keep teenage students' attention are to introduce novelty, tap into emotion, and present a meaningful curriculum. Dopamine, a neurotransmitter that emits feelings of pleasure, is released into the brain when something novel occurs. Brains of all ages are attracted to novelty, but to the teenage brain it is nirvana. They thrive on it. The new, the different, and the unusual are what spark their attention.

Emotion also plays an important role in capturing and keeping student attention. When the brain perceives something as being fun or pleasurable, it releases dopamine and endorphins. Conventional wisdom and past practice have traditionally led teachers to keep emotion out of the classroom. The thought was that if you let excitement, passion, and anger loose in the classroom, pandemonium would reign. Current research now points to emotion as an important memory builder. Connect information to emotion, and it takes the express train to the brain.

Highly emotional times are referred to as *flashbulb moments*. Our brains take an exciting or disturbing picture of the information, place, or event and sear it into our minds. Your first day of kindergarten, a special birthday party, the disaster of September 11 are all examples of flashbulb moments. In the classroom, do not actively seek high emotion; instead, encourage feelings of contentment, satisfaction, and amusement to get student attention.

The third way to draw attention is through content that is meaningful to students. What teacher hasn't heard a thousand times "Why do I need to know this?" Students pay attention and assign value to work that they consider meaningful. Understanding that there is a reason to learn something because of future careers, bargain shopping, or serving the community will make course content seem relevant to the adolescent's life.

Attention getters:

- Dress like a character in Tom Sawyer to introduce the book.
- Tell the story of your first date before you discuss *Romeo and Juliet*.
- Invite a construction worker to talk about how he or she uses math or computers as part of daily work.
- Use word cues such as "Hey, guys, listen up" or "Everybody stick with me."
- Pause before the most important parts of a story or instruction.
- Raise or lower your voice.
- Use humor, whether your own or others' cartoons and funny stories.
- Show a film, but don't dim the lights too much—it's an opportunity to doze.
- Change locations (move to different spots in the room to speak)—the brain loves to follow movement.
- Hang posters, such as pictures of a human cell or Mount Rushmore—a picture is worth a thousand words to the brain.
- Bring in a suitcase of props to stimulate creative writing. Don't, however, use props that need to be passed around the room, and don't use animals—they become distracters rather than attention getters.
- Have everyone bring in a snack to share, or provide popcorn.
- Role-play—for example, as an introduction to making laws, have pairs of students reenact an argument that they had with their parents (perhaps over the car).

Once you have students' attention, do not expect to keep it forever. Even adults who are listening to the most interesting of speeches will let their minds drift after a while. As a rule of thumb, you can maintain students' attention 1 minute for every year old they are; that is, 15-year-olds should be able to pay attention for 15 minutes.

Not surprisingly, that number needs to be reduced for at-risk kids. You can expect to keep the at-risk students' attention for approximately

7 to 8 minutes in high school and 5 to 6 minutes in middle school. This is a challenge in the regular school classroom, where you have a mix of students who can easily stay on task for 15 minutes and students who are challenged to stay on task for 7 minutes. There is no simple solution; some kind of compromise is necessary to meet the needs of all students.

PROCESSING TIME

After paying attention, the brain needs time to process what it has learned. The brain can either pay attention to information or process information, but it cannot do both at once. Teachers who continually have to teach and reteach material are usually not giving students time to process. If the material is difficult and unfamiliar, students will need 5 to 7 minutes to process after 15 minutes of instruction; if the material is easy and familiar, a shorter amount of time—like 1 to 2 minutes—is all that's required.

Processing time can be content driven, or it can be divergent. Conducting a class discussion, working in pairs, doing a worksheet, and journaling are all academic ways to process information. Doing an unrelated activity can also enhance processing. Casual conversation, passing classes, and eating lunch all give the brain time to make sense of information.

The brain processes information unconsciously and for much longer than we are aware. Fifteen-year-old Debra provides a good example of this. She was trying to figure out what to write about for a 10th-grade English assignment that asked her to describe a special gift that she had been given and what it meant to her. "I couldn't think of anything that was important or personal." She kept mulling it over and over in her mind. Then, while eating lunch and talking to her friends, the idea came to her. "I wrote about my older cousin who was killed in an automobile accident. She taught me to use deodorant when I was 11." Debra's brain had processed a sweet and touching moment that she had had with her cousin.

Processing activities:

- Instruct students to journal (writing requires complex thinking).
- Have students select the most valuable piece of information they just learned.

- Conduct a class discussion either as a large group or in small groups or pairs.
- Individually generate examples of the content taught.
- Ask students to explain how information relates to them.
- Summarize the content.
- Create a question about the new knowledge.
- Design a concept web.
- Add additional information to what was presented.
- Periodically provide nonacademic processing time.

INSTRUCTIONAL STRATEGIES

There is a big difference between a seventh grader's brain and a 12th grader's brain. The seventh grader will jump in the teacher's chair as soon as she leaves the room and take a spin but be shocked when the teacher reenters the room and yells at him. The 12th grader decides that it's not worth the trouble and stays seated. The seventh grader will become frustrated and mad when given a difficult homework assignment; the 12th grader sits down and begins working and calls a friend for help if it's too difficult to tackle alone.

Elementary school children look at the world concretely; manipulatives assist in addition and subtraction, and social studies revolves around the familiar, their community and state. As the frontal lobes mature during middle school and high school, students begin problem solving, synthesizing, and deducting information without the support of hands-on materials. Experience increases the ability to engage in abstract thought. Often, the at-risk student has had fewer experiences than his or her peers have had and thus has difficulty thinking abstractly. Therefore, more hands-on materials mixed with abstract problems will be necessary for learning to occur with the at-risk student.

Multiple Intelligences

The theory of multiple intelligences offers a wonderful and comprehensive way to present instruction and assess learning. Howard Gardner has proposed a theory of eight and a half intelligences, with each intelligence being located in different parts of the brain. Instructional strategies can be designed to appeal to each of the different intelligences to enable students to store information using a variety of pathways to the brain. This then makes it easier for them to retrieve information. The following is an example of using a multiple-intelligences approach to teach a unit on the book *The Diary of Anne Frank*:

Verbal/linguistic: Read and discuss the book.

Logical/mathematical: Map the paths that the German and Japanese armies took during World War II.

Visual/spatial: Watch a movie about Anne Frank.

Bodily/kinesthetic: Role-play parts of the story.

Musical: Listen to music of that era, or learn a Jewish dance.

Naturalist: This category does not fit neatly into this unit, but don't worry if not every intelligence fits into every unit. Be careful, however, not to go too long without including an intelligence.

Interpersonal: Do a group WebQuest (more on this later in the chapter) about the Holocaust. Because intelligences can overlap, this activity also incorporates linguistic and logical intelligences.

Intrapersonal: Individually make a timeline of the events in the war.

Existentialist (the one-half intelligence): Discuss factors that lead to genocide.

Differentiated Instruction

One way to ensure good and passing grades is through a differentiated curriculum. Elementary schools have been quick to grasp and implement this philosophy. It is more challenging at the secondary school level, partially because of the large number of students that the secondary education teacher has during the day. Still, it is the wave of the future. The point of differentiating curriculum is to offer different routes to learning. Realize that an entire year's curriculum cannot be differentiated overnight; so, revising one unit a semester or year is a goal worth pursuing.

Differentiation can be done in three ways:

1. content—what students learn, such as skills and concepts;
2. process—activities to assist the learner in making sense of the content; and

3. product—the multitude of ways that students can demonstrate their learning.

Other Instructional Strategies

Cooperative learning groups. The research on cooperative learning groups is strongly convincing; students benefit from working with peers. Careful structuring of groups enhances their probability of success and increases student satisfaction. Giving each student a specific responsibility and having individual and group accountability lend organization to cooperative learning groups.

Varied books and texts. Using the same book in literature or the same history textbook for all students will not meet all of their needs. At times, it is appropriate to individualize by interest level, ability level, or content when selecting books.

Choice. Let students choose the medium, whether it is a video, a book, an interview, or art through which they want to study a particular content. Choice is power, and we teachers don't often like to give it up. Teenagers will benefit if we do. I acknowledge that there are realistic restraints to offering options. The No Child Left Behind Act makes offering choices difficult; teachers are constrained within a restrictive curriculum.

Learning contracts. Contracts are an effective way to reduce student stress; they put everyone on the same page as to what exactly is expected to receive a particular letter grade. Write into the contract requirements for quality as well as quantity.

Varied support systems. Explore the possibility of peer tutoring, adult tutoring, mentoring, and mixed grade-level tutoring.

Interest groups. Mysteries, nature, computers, technology, drama, rock or classical music, sculpture, math, journalism, Europe, Middle East, football, basketball, retail, history, civics, biology, and so on. Occasionally group students by their personal interests.

Varied graphic organizers. Graphic organizers are also supported by research. When we pair verbal (lecture or discussion) with a graphic, we enhance memory. There are endless options when it comes to graphic organizers: KWL (what I *know*, what I *want* to know, what I *learned*), chain of events, and Venn diagrams are but a few. The beauty of graphic organizers is that each can be made simpler or more complex to meet the needs of the learner.

Independent study. This strategy gives students an opportunity to work at their own academic levels. The following is an example of independent study tiered by Bloom's taxonomy: Some students recall information (knowledge) about the war in Iraq; other students analyze the impetus behind going and staying in the war (analysis and evaluation); and other students review ads from television and magazines to identify propaganda techniques, and they make a poster illustrating the various techniques (application).

Study buddies. Social interaction motivates adolescents because they want to be with their peers. This strategy kills two birds with one stone by providing a social connection during learning.

Jigsaw. Divide the tasks of researching and writing about an American hero among three students in the following manner: One student tackles the hero's early life; the next, the hero's adult life; and the third student, the hero's professional contributions.

Small group instruction. Flexible grouping is the key to success. Inflexibility may be why grouping has failed in the past. Don't allow placement in a group to become a life sentence for students. Grouping students for instruction can be done in a variety of ways: by interest, ability, or learning style.

WebQuest. This inquiry-based activity requires that students gather at least part of the information for a project or assignment from the Internet. WebQuests are effective ways for students to research and problem-solve such topics as career exploration and global warming. It's best if the teacher designs the WebQuest at first.

Promote mastery of essential content. Automaticity (mastery) comes from repeatedly engaging in an activity, wiring the same neurons to fire over and over again. As the synaptic connections become stronger, the task requires less brain power, enabling the brain to take on more-complex tasks. For instance, once you learn your math facts, your brain's energy is free to move on to more challenging math equations.

Strategies for Products and Assessment

Conducting assessments is a time-honored practice in education. Originally designed to assist teachers in making good decisions concerning their students, they are now too often relegated to the unpleasant and unworthy job of sorting. Which students learned? Which did not? Which teacher is doing his or her job? Which is not?

Traditional multiple choice, essay, and true-false tests are all ways to evaluate work, but alternate ways to assess and give feedback may be friendlier to at-risk students. At-risk students often shut down from stress when given traditional tests. The following list is of performance-based assessment tools that can give teachers a clear picture of student achievement:

- Design an advertisement.
- Make a videotape.
- Make a speech.
- Write a book review.
- Write an advice column.
- Paraphrase.
- Give oral reports.
- Create a jingle.
- Collect recipes.
- Write and perform a rap.
- Write riddles.
- Discuss.
- Write brochures.
- Publish a newspaper.
- Make an audiotape.
- Play game shows.
- Create a crossword puzzle.
- Write how-to guides.
- Keep a journal.
- Conduct interviews.
- Summarize.
- Set personal goals.
- Write slogans.
- Self-assess.
- Write fairy tales.
- Make predictions.
- Design a maze.
- Compare.

- Outline.
- Take a walking tour.
- Make a matrix.
- Problem-solve.
- Analogize.
- Conduct surveys.
- Make a time line.
- Trivia.
- Sing.
- Chart.
- Give demonstrations.
- Graph maps.
- Invent a code.
- Conduct mock trials.
- Design a flow chart.
- Do a photo essay.
- Make a computer game.
- Keep diaries.
- Draw.
- Design board games.
- Illustrate.
- Find metaphors.
- Make a website.
- Conduct panel discussions.
- Draw cartoons.
- Make collages.
- Identify superstitions.
- Produce a comic book.
- Pantomime.
- Produce commercials.
- Dance.
- Establish contracts.
- Practice improvisation.
- Make a poster.
- Role-play.
- Design a mobile.
- Create simulations.

- Diagram.
- Write sequels.
- Do research.
- Make sculptures.
- Create scrapbooks.
- Design PowerPoint presentations.
- Engage in debate.
- Write poetry.
- Write a character sketch.
- Experiment.
- Compose lyrics.

Lesson Plan Matrix

The following chart is a wonderful way to combine multiple intelligences with different levels of thinking (Bloom's taxonomy) to achieve higher orders of learning. Teachers are continually criticized for focusing instruction and questions on just knowledge and comprehension, both of which are examples of lower levels of thinking. Application, analysis, synthesis, and evaluation tap into higher levels of thinking; they enable students to think abstractly and become lifelong learners. Using this chart helps teachers access all levels of learning with the various learning styles in multiple intelligences. Process and product are part of this lesson plan matrix.

LANGUAGE DEVELOPMENT

Jake told me about riding in the car with his 14-year-old daughter who was yammering on and on about her day at school. She paused to take a breath midsentence; she furrowed her brow and said, "What am I talking about?" Even she didn't know!

The ability to communicate and articulate thoughts, if encouraged, increases greatly during the teenage years. Language is mainly located in the left hemisphere of the brain, but when we speak, neurons fire all over the prefrontal lobes. Two modules in the brain, Wernicke's area and Broca's area, are responsible for interpreting what others say and for changing thoughts into words. During the teenage years, Wernicke's

Table 2.1. Multiple Intelligences (Bloom's Taxonomy)

Knowledge Know, repeat, list, define, label, recommend	Comprehension Summarize, explain, paraphrase, identify	Application Exhibit, apply, solve, practice, experiment, interview	Analysis Test, interpret, examine	Synthesis Create, compose, make, plan, design	Evaluation Judge, compare, criticize
		Verbal/Linguistic: Brainstorm, read, write			
		Math/Logical: Graph, cause and effect			
		Bodily/Kinesthetic: Role-play, dance			
		Visual/Spatial: Poster, video, drawing			

(continued)

Table 2.1. *(continued)*

Knowledge *Know, repeat, list, define, label recommend*	Comprehension *Summarize, explain, paraphrase, identify*	Application *Exhibit, apply, solve, practice, experiment, interview*	Analysis *Test, interpret, examine*	Synthesis *Create, compose, make, plan, design*	Evaluation *Judge, compare, criticize*
Musical: Rhyme, song, dance					
Interpersonal: Cooperative groups, interview, game					
Intrapersonal: Individual research, journal, scrapbook					
Naturalist: Animals, plants, ecology, environment					

area and Broca's areas become fully developed, as does the corpus callosum, which allows communication between the two hemispheres, and the hippocampus, which is responsible for transferring short-term memory into long-term memory. The brain is hardwired for sophisticated language skills.

Reading, discussion, and life experiences facilitate the teenager's ability to understand advanced language skills such as symbolism, irony, and sarcasm. Teenagers enjoy engaging in interesting and provocative conversations; they are finally old enough to catch all the innuendoes and humor.

At-risk teenagers need support and guidance to develop their potential in the language arts. Traditional literature requirements such as *Macbeth* and *The Illiad* may not be the best medium to meet their interests or needs. To be effective, reading and writing curriculum needs to be at the correct academic and interest level of the student. This often means age-appropriate interest at a lower reading level. There is an excellent variety of adolescent literature available today; teachers should not feel hesitant to explore suitable alternatives.

Interestingly, as teenagers make progress in developing their language skills, some of their communication skills deteriorate. Teens provide less information to adults, and what they do say is often colored with attitude. Teenagers have a triple disadvantage on the communication circuit: They misread emotions; their emotional amygdala controls the brain; and their prefrontal cortex is in an underdeveloped state.

Deborah Yurgelun-Todd and associates conducted compelling research on the teenage brain. Adults and teens were given the same photograph to view, a picture of a woman with fear on her face. One hundred percent of the adults in the study correctly identified the emotion as fear, but only half of the teens identified fear as the emotion. Instead, they suggested that the woman showed shock or surprise.

Curious about these findings, Yurgelun-Todd expanded the research in hopes of discovering the reasons for the differing responses. She repeated the experiment but this time used fMRI to scan participants' brains as they viewed the picture. She found that all of the adults used their frontal lobes, the part of the brain used for making decisions and analyzing, when they interpreted the picture.

The teens, however, used their amygdalas, the emotional center of the brain. No wonder their responses were different—their brains function differently.

These results explain why teens make so many misinterpretations and misunderstandings: They rely on an emotional part of their brains to interpret body and facial language and speech. Researchers surmise that interpreting these communication elements is a learned skill; it's not something that people inherit. Teens are in the process of learning what smirks, shrugs, and stares mean.

How does this play out in real life? When a teacher stares at a teen while waiting for an answer, the teen interprets it as though the teacher hates him or her. In the school lunchroom, a teen across the room turns and looks in the other direction, and another teen interprets it as a signal that no one else is welcome at the table. Even adults sometimes revert back to using this part of the brain, particularly when under stress. The upset teacher whose son is picked up for drunk driving may misread a colleague's comment or stare as a criticism of his or her parenting or family.

In the teen brain, the amygdala is in charge, not the frontal lobes, which makes conversations potentially volatile. A calm comment is met with a storm of verbal abuse. An innocent question such as "Are you reading that book?" sets off a stream of tears and foot stomping as a teenager yells in response, "You are unfair. You don't like me!" Because adolescents are such emotional communicators, it is easy to make light of their problems. Teachers with good communication skills can set a good example for the teenager to follow, or they can at least mollify an obstinate conversation.

When you converse with teens, it is important to respect their ideas, even when they seem trivial. Resist the temptation to set teens straight. Just listen and maybe even commiserate with comments such as "That must be a hard way to start your day," to let them know that you understand. Do not trivialize their concerns—at this point in their life, these are major worries.

Communication tips for conversing with teens:

- Listen to them more than you talk to them.
- Begin statements with *I* instead of *you* to diminish defensiveness.

- Be open to learning from students, and let them occasionally instruct you.
- Stay focused on the conversation, and resist the temptation to interrupt with your own stories.
- Accept their opinions and ideas even when they radically differ from yours.
- Be an active listener, and periodically ask questions to show interest.
- Show empathy, and identify with their point of view.
- Withhold advice unless they ask you for it; they want to solve their own problems.
- Allow them to discuss whatever topic they wish.
- Be pleasant and stay positive, or else end the conversation.
- Avoid generalizations.
- Ask questions that require more than one-word responses.

CHAPTER 3

Staying in and Thriving in School

Disorganized, unmotivated, and hoping that no one will notice. Teenagers are transforming from dependent children into independent adults, and everybody involved hopes that along the way, teens will earn their high school diplomas, get a hair cut, and find jobs.
Did you know that . . .

- the newly developing teenage brain is responsible for a forgetful and disorganized glitch?
- teenagers give complicated and convoluted solutions to simple problems?
- transferring from middle school to high school is stressful and threatening?
- truancy is the first sign that teachers have that a student is at risk of dropping out of school?

HOMEWORK AND STUDY SKILLS

The computer was downloading songs from iTunes; music was blaring; and someone was singing slightly off-key throughout the house. Suddenly, the moment was interrupted by a mother shouting, "Jeffrey what are you doing?" Jeffery replied, with mild annoyance, "I'm doing my homework." Jeffrey had physical evidence to back up his claim; he sat surrounded by his math book, paper, and pencils. Still, the operative term *doing* was up for discussion.

Forgetful, disorganized, and late for everything but dinner . . . all teenagers can seem like whirling dervishes. Middle schooler after middle schooler forgets to do or hand in homework. One girl left her textbook at a friend's house and didn't remember to get it for a week. Absentminded teens are the norm, not the exception. At-risk teenagers tend to extend these traits from middle school into high school. Disorganization and forgetfulness become compounded because at-risk teens often lack parental support at home. There is no adult to remind them to do their homework or return the note to school.

This flakiness is related to the changes going on in the brain. Remembering and organizing require a temporary mental workspace—a working memory—that develops throughout adolescence. Furthermore, all of the development and new capabilities of the brain make it difficult for reminders to stick. Teens can literally forget what a teacher or their parents just said. Students forget their books at school when there's homework, and they forget their books at home when they need them at school. And just when you're ready to offer them some help, they turn and inform you that "it's all your fault!"

One of the biggest frustrations for teachers and parents alike is probably one of the explainations for why homework is never turned in: "It was only worth five points." This dismissal of an assignment brings up issues of responsibility and dependability, and it ignores the potential of just handing in homework to easily raise a grade.

Adolescent brains are really not prepared to be perfect. Be forewarned—you'll need to find the balance between making exceptions and letting teens suffer the consequences. There will be times when you give them a second chance (everybody forgets something, sometimes) and when they will just have to lose the points on an assignment.

When they do remember something important, praise them. It's amazing how often praise and kind words are overlooked during adolescence. Simple comments such as "It looks like you worked hard on that paper" or "You really seem to understand math" are music to teens' ears. If need be, consciously decide that you are going to say one positive things to each student every week.

Reminders are important, so help teens keep a calendar and use a school planner—these establish great life skills. School administrators can help here. A principal at one middle school randomly went to one room each week, checked three students' planners, and threw a class pizza party if they were up to date. This was a strong incentive to start a good habit.

Teach students how to take notes. In middle school, it is preferable if all teachers at a grade level are on the same page and promote one note-taking style. It can be KWL, double column, or outline—the style itself isn't important; rather, it's the ability to practice it in a variety of classes. Consistency and continuity in note taking allow students to master a style.

Heads up: If you are lecturing and expecting students to take notes, pause and give them time to write. Both listening and writing require teens' undivided attention, and one skill always suffers when they are combined.

My two favorite note-taking styles are double column (also known as the Cornell method) and forming questions according to subheadings in a text. Double-column note taking consists of dividing a paper into two columns: one two thirds the width of the paper and the other, one third the width. Students take notes in the wide column and later write questions about the notes in the narrow column. A strip at the bottom of the page may be used to summarize the page of notes or to draw a graphic representation of the notes. As such, students encode new information in at least three ways. Double-column notes can be used with a lecture or a textbook.

The second form of note taking works best when taking notes from a textbook. It requires that students first develop a question for each subheading in the text they are reading. As they read the section, they jot down answers to the question. For instance, if a section is entitled "The Beginning of World War II," the question might be, "What caused the war to begin?" The notes that answer the question might include "German invasion of Poland," "ineffective resolution of World War I," and "Hitler."

At-risk students need direct instruction on how to budget study time. Having them keep a record of how they spend their time after school is a good first step to a reality check. They are often amazed to find that they actually studied only 7 minutes (during commercials) instead of 30 minutes (the length of time their book was in front of them).

Study skill strategies:

- Study in a quiet place with no television, CD player, or radio turned on.

- Build short breaks into your study time; take a 5-minute break every 20 to 30 minutes.
- Study during daylight—it's 50% more productive than studying once the sun sets.
- Review every subject within 1 day of learning it to increase your memory of it.
- Prioritize assignments and stick to your schedule.
- Estimate how long each assignment will take before beginning it.

Mr. Rayburt assigned his seventh-grade students a 170-page book to read over 2 weeks (a totally reasonable, age-appropriate expectation). The night before the book was due, one student, John, found himself with 150 pages left to read. His mom and dad found him in a state of panic with no viable solution close at hand. His emotion-driven response was "I hate reading and I hate school!"

John is evidence that middle schoolers are not good at estimating how much they need to read each night. The following two formulas will help them figure out just how many minutes they need to read each night to finish a book within an allotted period.

1. First, figure out how many pages you need to read a night. Divide the number of days you have to complete the book (in this instance, 14 days) by the number of pages in the book (170 pages), which means that you need to read about 12 pages each evening.
2. Second, figure out how fast you read.
   - Read silently for 6 minutes.
   - Count the number of pages that you read during those 6 minutes (in this example, let's say that you read three pages).
   - Multiply the number of pages read by 10 to calculate the number of pages that you can read in an hour (30 pages per hour).
3. Finally, estimate how much time you will have to budget for reading your nightly pages (about 70 minutes).

In middle school, homework can become the battlefield upon which teachers and students wage war. Often, the at-risk student does not receive support from home; add to that a disorganized brain and you have a recipe for disaster. Reducing the amount of homework (the research on its academic advantages for middle schoolers is controversial) can reduce your frustration and, more important, their stress by eliminating a source of conflict. Another option is to offer students two or three late passes on homework each semester to reduce their stress level. This is not a pass to forgo the work forever but to delay it for 1 or 2 days.

PSEUDOSTUPIDITY: MAKING SIMPLE ASSIGNMENTS COMPLEX

Making simple tasks complex is a preoccupation of most young and old at-risk adolescents. Middle school teachers see pseudostupidity on a daily, if not hourly, basis. Teachers assign a relatively simple assignment, and before you know it, the adolescent has blown it all out of proportion. Instead of completing a simple math equation, he or she reworks it as a problem that would bring Einstein to his knees. Teens' awkward analyses of problems and situations lie in the modifications going on in their frontal lobes. Abstract thinking is developing, but young adolescents aren't very good at managing it, which results in inept attempts to apply abstract thought.

Teenagers also make the simple complex as they navigate social situations. A good example of this involves Kevin, an eighth grader. One teacher described him as a kid who "didn't quite fit in anywhere—not bad enough to be one of the bad, not cool enough to run with the cool kids, and not smart enough to be one of the brainiacs." Kevin once brought oregano to school with hopes of selling it as pot. He didn't really have a group to hang with, and selling the "pot" was his attempt to get into one. Sadly, his group of choice was the bad group. From the get-go, Kevin was not a good drug dealer. He loudly talked about the pot; teachers overheard him; and he and his oregano were taken to the office. Kevin's rough attempt to make his social life better was ill-planned, and the consequences left him in deep trouble. The fact that some of his classmates were hauled to the office for attempting to buy the "pot" compounded Kevin's social status problems.

Everyone (every adult, anyway) knows that the simplest approach—being yourself—is the best way to make friends. Young adolescents and at-risk adolescents opt for more complicated solutions. They go to extremes to make friends, trying to impress others by being too loud or too strange, often attracting a troublesome group or generating the opposite response to what they were seeking.

How should you handle pseudostupidity and overcomplications? Be patient. Stay calm because adolescents won't. Be hands-on. Continue to give them practice solving complex problems, such as "What should our school community do about creating a green environment?" or "What do you think about immigration into the United States?" Encourage them to enroll in challenging but not frustrating classes in school; they will grow better brains through active involvement in areas that they find interesting.

TRANSITIONING TO MIDDLE SCHOOL AND HIGH SCHOOL

Transitioning to middle school and high school can be threatening and scary. These are major life events for adolescents, and in many ways their brains are not equipped to handle the change. The new school means juggling more teachers, more rooms, and more work. Figuring which hallways connect to which classrooms requires a map and a good friend. Speaking of which, teens may find themselves without any close friends in class or even during lunch (much scarier). Their worries and fears seem to exponentially escalate as the first day of school approaches.

Schools often offer opportunities for families to visit ahead of time. You should encourage families to take advantage of this. If your school doesn't have a day for incoming students to visit, talk to your principal about arranging one. Find out what is stressing your students, and try to alleviate the worry with active engagement. Perhaps set aside class time the first week of school for students to practice opening their lockers over and over again. (Dreams of being unable to remember locker combinations still haunt some adults!) As has been said already, familiarity breeds comfort. Anxiety tends to dramatically decrease after the first month or even the first week of the school year.

DROPOUTS

"I hate school."

   "I'm flunking."

"I want a job."

"My teachers hate me."

All of these quotes are from students contemplating dropping out of school. In response to the question of why her school had such high dropout rates, one teacher answered, "The girls want babies, and the boys want jobs." Such statements are indicative of consistent themes in the perception of school life and postschool life that drive the decision for students to drop out.

Approximately 15% of Americans do not graduate from high school, and there is concern that those numbers are on the rise. Although the facts are disconcerting, it should not be surprising that the lion's share of that 15% belongs to minority students and to students of low socio-economic status. Between 87% and 92% of low-income students are not proficient in reading. One third of Latino students perform below grade level, which leads to dropout rates of a staggering 22%. In fact, 82% of prisoners are high school dropouts. These unsettling statistics are a sampling of the disturbing achievement gap in our nation.

The future impact of dropping out on the individual and society is multifaceted. Lost earnings and unrealized tax revenue from students dropping out of school is enormous. Evidence of economic impact can be seen in statistics on annual income. Teenagers who drop out of school can expect to make $16,000 annually; students with a GED, $18,000; and high school graduates, $20,000. These are all incomes — even the high school graduate — that constrain an individual to the poverty zone. If a student completes post–high school training or college, his or her potential income skyrockets. There is a high correlation between level of education and earning power.

Safety issues, identity development, and self-esteem are all negatively influenced for the student who drops out. Society expects its citizens to receive that diploma; many feelings of inferiority result from failing to meet society's expectations.

School warning signs of potential dropouts:

- Academic failure
- Frequent tardiness
- Absenteeism
- Learning at 2 or more years below average age for grade

- Truancy (the teacher's first sign of dropout)
- Behavior problems
- Low reading ability
- Frequent changes of school
- Lack of friends or having friends much older or younger
- Nonparticipation in extracurricular activities
- Serious physical or emotional problems
- Delinquency
- Feelings of not belonging
- Dysfunctional family
- Low socioeconomic status
- Financial concerns (Hispanics and Latinos in particular dropout to help their families)
- Pregnancy

Becka made it through five semesters of high school when she dropped out. She was one credit short (a government class) of walking across the stage at graduation. The school principal and counselor did not let her go quietly into the night; they encouraged her to pick up the last credit at an alternative school. She went there, but her attendance was sporadic. Conferences with the director and teachers at the alternative school about the importance of completing high school had little impact on her decision. She seemed determined to be defiant even though she was hurting only herself. Eight years later, Becka is still a credit short and scrapes by as a cashier at an all night gas mart.

Stories like Becka's are not uncommon. The workings of the teenage mind often eliminate rational and logical thought and replace them with stubborn and rebellious behavior. The following are suggestions for working with potential dropouts:

- Having future teachers attend preservice teacher education programs that prepare them to work with at-risk students.
- Linking social services with schools—medical, social, and mental. It takes a village to raise a teenager.
- Mentoring—request volunteers from the community, or pair at-risk high school mentors with at-risk elementary students.

- Offering tutors—receiving extra academic assistance from adults, peers, and cross-age students helps at-risk teens from falling behind in classes.
- Ensuring the ability to complete homework during out-of-school suspension.
- Establishing summer school classes to help students make up failed classes and stay on course for graduation.
- Curbing the practice of automatic failure of a semester if a student is absent 10 days.
- Providing on-site day care for girls with babies.
- Using peer mediation and conflict resolution for handling issues such as truancy, instead of resorting to the juvenile court system.
- Offering school-to-work programs—opportunities to shadow professionals and participate in internships are strong motivators and help crystallize career goals.
- Involvement in extracurricular activities—an overinvolvement in activities can be harmful at the elementary level, but for the middle school and high school student, it's all positive.
- Recommending alternative schools and GED programs when appropriate.

CHAPTER 4

An Emotional Commotion

Emotional commotion—what teenager can't create one? Emotions rule during the teenage years. Anger, sadness, and frustration combine to make a toxic concoction of emotional confusion. Add to it changing hormones and brain renovations, and teenagers and their teachers are in for a rocky ride.

Did you know that . . .

- the brain of a younger adolescent differs greatly from that of an older adolescent?
- mothers routinely underestimate the amount of stress that their teenagers are under?
- teenagers do not have the brain hardware to make good decisions?
- the brain and puberty set the stage for mood swings in girls?
- transformations in the brain lead to teens' believing that they are indestructible

BAD DECISION MAKING

Andy provides an example of not thinking before doing. After wearing out his welcome at regular high school, he was attending the local alternative school. Angry and resentful of his past teachers and principal at the high school, he called in a bomb threat. Unfortunately, his reputation and cell phone number preceded him. The school secretary recognized the cell phone number (compliments of other not-so-alarming prank calls), and within a matter of minutes, he and his cell phone were picked up by the local police. Andy had made a bad decision.

Teens are known for making bad decisions; it is a skill that they continually hone. Decision making is one skill that requires careful negotiation in the fully developed frontal lobes. The brain of an early adolescent differs greatly from that of a late adolescent, in anatomy, biochemistry, and physiology, which makes good decision making particularly tricky. Unfortunately, the at-risk brain often functions like an early adolescent brain well into its twenties. At-risk frontal lobes really can't tell the difference between a good decision and a bad decision.

Opportunities to make age-appropriate decisions help teenagers learn decision-making skills. Some teachers have difficulty giving up control in their classroom; they want to decide what is studied, how it's studied, and when. Instead, they should periodically let teens start making their own decisions in the classroom (while still keeping the safety net handy, they should offer students choice on content (e.g., writing topics, books to be read, current events to discuss), process (e.g., read, write, watch a video, create a drawing, reenact a play), and product (e.g., poster, debate, interview, game). "Practice makes perfect" is a conventional wisdom that can help teachers keep perspective on teenage decision making.

At-risk teens need direct instruction in decision making. The following six skills can be incorporated into lesson plans to provide many chances for students to learn this skill.

1. Identify the problem or issue.
2. Identify various ways to solve the problem.
3. Spot problems that you may face in trying to solve the problem.
4. Find ways to handle any obstacles.
5. Rank the best way to solve the problem.
6. Choose and implement the best solution.

STRESS

A high school English teacher was tired of hearing her students complain about how "stressed out" they were. To start a discussion on this topic, she had them write about the stressors in their lives. One girl wrote, "Every night, I go home and take care of my little brother and sister. They are only 10 and 11, so they need somebody to make dinner and help them read at night. Thursday evenings and on the weekend, I work at a restaurant. I take car orders; it gets pretty hectic. Sometimes, the manager wants me to work extra hours. I've got to do it—I have a car and I need the money. Last week, I got an oil change. I know I should have done it sooner, but I was short on cash. And then I have homework. I want to do well in school, but sometimes it just piles up on me."

After reading the compositions, the teacher confided to the class that she was surprised at the multiple stressors present in their lives. In an effort to reduce their stress, the teacher compromised on a deadline for one of their assignments. Later, she said, "You could actually feel the stress in the room fade when I told them the good news."

Small and moderate amounts of stress are good. Without stress, we would fall asleep in class and daydream while driving. When an individual is moderately stressed, adrenaline is released into the body, which becomes alert and ready to adjust and react to situations. It directs one's attention and enhances one's memory.

Adolescents, however, have a great vulnerability to life stresses. The body first releases adrenalin when it feels stress, energizing and invigorating it. This activates a spurt of energy, which may help tackle the stressor and, ultimately, be a stress reducer. However, if stress persists, the steroid hormone cortisol is released. Cortisol stays in the body much too long. It causes the immune system to fall apart (which is why we get sick when we're under a great deal of stress); it increases heart rate and blood pressure (hand trembling, tension headaches, and anxiety are side effects); and remembering is difficult. In the midst of a verbal fight, it's hard to think of a perfect comeback; during important exams, answers to test questions pop into one's head only after turning in the test.

Once stressed, teens require a more lengthy recovery time than do adults. Teenage girls are particularly at risk. Progesterone, which is released in larger amounts with puberty, lets cortisol run rampant. Once a teenage girl becomes stressed, it is very difficult to get her physically and mentally under control.

Stress in school comes from a variety of places: between the teacher and the students, from academics, and from peers. Stressors from outside of school include family, work, and neighborhood tensions. Many at-risk students are particularly susceptible to stressors outside of school. Impoverished neighborhoods hold a high incidence of crime, drug abuse, and gang activity—an atmosphere that results in students feeling unsafe, insecure, and stressed. As teachers, we need to help them reduce stress.

Teenagers are often much more stressed than what their teachers and parents realize. The following is a list of ways to help teenagers reduce stress levels at school:

- Encourage physical exercise and sports. They release chemicals that increase happiness and reduce stress.
- Talk with teens about academic worries.
- Compliment them.
- Use humor.
- Be a role model of self-control and appropriate coping skills.
- Encourage them to seek help from you outside of class.
- Don't expect perfection. Assure teens with such comments as "Giving it a try is what is important" and "I can see you worked hard on this."
- Use competition carefully and ensure that everyone has a chance to succeed.
- Suggest meditation and deep breathing.
- Explain that drugs and alcohol increase stress and reduce the body's ability to employ healthy coping skills.
- Refer teens to the school counselor or professional help if you believe that their stress is a serious problem.

Encourage these coping skills for teens when they are outside of school:

- Spend time with family and friends.
- Participate in an extracurricular activity.
- Volunteer.
- Write in a journal.

- Exercise.
- Read books or magazines that make you feel good.
- Avoid watching the news for a month (it can be depressing).
- Talk to someone about your feelings (e.g., family, friend, counselor).
- Avoid stressful relationships.

ACTIONS AND CONSEQUENCES

Teenagers try the very souls of adults with some of their actions: ignoring homework, underage drinking, hanging with an unsavory gang. There seems to be a disconnect in the teenage mind between their present actions and future consequences.

Neuroscientist Deborah Yurgelun-Todd explained the inner working of the teenage brain by saying, "Good judgment is learned, but you can't learn it if you don't have the necessary hardware." Adolescents don't have the necessary hardware to make good choices. Overproduction, pruning, and myelination are fine-tuning the frontal lobes, but the brainpower necessary for good decision making is still in its infancy. Teens simply aren't capable of always forecasting the consequences of their behaviors. Bludgeoning them with guilt over past transgressions has about as much effect as reprimanding a two-year-old for breaking a dish while trying to unload a dishwasher.

Adolescents are also challenged by the concept of time. It's been said that a middle schooler defines the future as 3:00 p.m. (when school lets out). Such limited vision leads to shortsighted actions. A better understanding of time kicks in around age 14, but in the meantime it is very difficult for teens to understand the future consequences of their actions.

The more that teachers relate behaviors to immediate consequences, the better the chance that a teen will make the connection. For instance, a teenager can relate smoking to bad breath and stinky hair but will be lost by talk of lung cancer and emphysema. They need consequences that they can see and hear now. The abstract future consequences of a lifetime of smoking, where one doesn't get to play with one's grandchildren, may have meaning for the adult brain but are wasted on the teenage brain.

ARGUE AND ARGUE

Bryce, a seventh grader, was using a lighter on the school bus. When the bus driver caught the flickering sight of fire amid the sea of students, she stopped the bus and asked everyone, who was lighting matches? Without meaning to point guilt, everyone's eyes gravitated toward Bryce, who admitted to using the lighter and willingly handed it over to the driver.

Bryce was already in trouble, but his next actions cinched the deal. As the bus driver dropped him off at his stop, Bryce turned to the driver and demanded the lighter back. The bus driver, of course, refused. At this point, Bryce threatened legal action if she didn't return the lighter to him. After all, he explained, "It's mine." As the doors of the bus closed, so did Bryce's fate. The next day, Bryce had an early-morning conference in the principal's office, with his parents.

Teachers can expect an increase in arguments during middle school and high school. Homework, tests, in-class seat assignment . . . sometimes, it seems that adolescents will fight over anything and everything. Changes in the brain increase the likelihood of arguments between teens and teachers in two ways. First, teenagers are capable of understanding complex decision making, analytical thought, and reasoning. They want to know why the decision is made, not just what the decision is. They are no longer the children that blindly accept the adult's manifesto. Second, the emotional part of the brain is in charge so that argumentativeness, moodiness, and yelling prevail over serenity and tranquility. Teachers are bewildered by this behavior and wonder how much attitude they should tolerate, what ground they should hold, and what kind of classroom management they should effect.

Middle schoolers tend to comply with teachers' directives, assignments, and rationale. Be forewarned, though, that high schoolers are much less willing to concede in thought or deed. A young teen will reluctantly agree to sit down and start working on an assignment, but an older teen might consider the assignment rubbish and worthy of an argument.

Do not reduce yourself to the level of teens by arguing with them. They are not as mentally or emotionally mature as adults, and the difference becomes apparent during an argument. They are almost always compelled to continue a fight. When an argument arises, calmly and concisely state your views and then stop.

If a teen's outburst goes along the lines of "I don't see why I have to get off the computer—Matt never has to get off the computer," do not take the time explaining the computer rules. The teen is trying to engage you in an argument. Instead, turn the tables and say, "Why do you think we have rules about the computer?" The typical response will be, "I don't know." Reply with "Then tell me what you do know." Continue this same phrase in response to each "I don't know." About 80% of the time, the teen will explain the rule to you and, in the process, calm down.

An alternative approach is to calmly yet firmly repeat your direction to turn off the computer. When the teen tries to draw you into an argument, continue to repeat your direction. A teen will quickly get the message that this directive is nonnegotiable.

If the teen persists in arguing, suggest that she or he continue the discussion with you after class. Worse comes to worse, the teen may need to leave the classroom. When students are removed from the classroom, it is key that they understand that they are welcome back once their behavior becomes appropriate.

CHALLENGING AUTHORITY

A group of high schools boys—Mike, Ben, and Tyler—skipped one class each week; it was always random which class they would choose. Mike would just say, "Let's get out of here," and the group would follow. Like clockwork, they would return to school before the next class period. They knew that they faced detention later, but for them the act of defiance was worth the punishment.

Teenagers will challenge almost everything that adults value. As irritating as it is, in moderation this defiance can actually be a good and normal thing; in excess, it is unacceptable and not to be tolerated. It's important to remember that teens that probe, debate, and throw in a doubtful scowl are not personally attacking the teacher or administrator.

Encourage independent thinking. When teens say that they want to discuss abortion or diversity, allow it. When they argue for the right to smoke on school grounds when they know that school policy is dead set against it, listen and let them know when a point makes some sense. These actions are usually a mixture of exploring their identity and a mini-rebellion—both are in the norm.

Unfortunately, teens often take challenging authority to an extreme and confront teachers, parents, and adults in inappropriate ways. Teens who call adults names, yell, and use profanity are crossing the line. Teachers who feel threatened and attempt to argue and undermine these actions and statements just set the stage for a full-blown rebellion. Let teens know that overt confrontation, such as cursing or taking swings at people, is not acceptable behavior. Suggest a cooldown period (anywhere from 10 minutes to an entire day) during which everyone agrees not to discuss a hot topic until heads have cooled.

IMPULSE CONTROL: GETTING MAD

During adolescence, the amygdala is in the driver's seat, and the frontal lobes seem to be on cruise control, oblivious to the raucous scenery. The connection between the amygdala and the frontal lobes is just beginning to strengthen. Until the process is completed, foolish and furious choices are a frequent occurrence. It's not fair to blame a teenager for a lack of emotional control, but it is his or her responsibility to try to gain control. Teachers can help. This is a window of opportunity for the teenager. Never will it be easier to learn to control fury, frustration, and impulse. Individuals who do not gain control over their negative emotions during adolescence turn into the adults with anger management issues.

Encourage teens to think before they speak or act. Be specific about what is tolerated and what is not: "You cannot call anyone names" and "Don't hit the wall." The more specific your mandate, the better it will be understood. Do not try to reason with a teen in the middle of an argument. Be patient and save the conversation for when things have cooled and calmed down.

If teens continue to fly out of control, follow through on consequences. Make sure the consequences are logical, and appropriately address the bad behavior. As you consider a proper consequence, remember that communication is the most effective way to change teenage behavior.

INDESTRUCTIBLE AND IMMORTAL

Teenagers have difficulty comprehending that bad things can happen to them; in their minds, they are sheltered from harm's way. Neuroscientists believe that this is due to the many changes experienced in the teenage brain. This oblivious mind-set explains the risky behavior they actively pursue, such as unprotected sex ("I won't get an STD"), driving recklessly ("I won't be injured or killed"), and smoking ("I won't get lung cancer").

The best defense against this type of behavior is to monitor and do our best to curb risky business. School curricula that include health topics such as STDs (among the industrialized nations, the United States has the highest rate of STDs; experts attribute it to educators' and parents' encouraging ignorance about them), contraception, and drug and alcohol prevention are meeting the immediate needs of teenagers. Open the door to conversation, but back it up with an adult perspective.

MOOD SWINGS

Molly cried inconsolably to her mother, "I have no friends. Nobody likes me, not anyone. I have no friends," and it didn't look like her river of tears would stop flowing any time soon. Then the phone rang. It was Whitney; she was wondering if Molly would like to come over. The tears immediately dried up, and Molly acted as though nothing had happened. Molly's mom shrugged her shoulders and thought to herself that another crisis had been averted.

The combination of brain development and inconsistent estrogen levels leaves the teenage girl swinging from being elated to being edgy on a daily basis. Mood swings are common in girls during the teenage years. Chemicals in the brain—norepinephrine and adrenaline (energizing), serotonin (calming), and dopamine (feeling good)—percolate in every-one, but during puberty, high levels of estrogen contribute to girls' mood swings. One moment, everything is wonderful in their world, and the next minute (and I do mean *minute*—girls' moods can change very quickly during adolescence), they think that they are ugly, have no friends, and are convinced that no one cares about or understands them.

Showing a bit of empathy and patience sets the stage for a more calm and peaceful existence. But again, you do not have to let mood swings be an excuse for unacceptable behavior. Keep your standards high and remind girls of appropriate behaviors.

HYPOCRISY

Adolescent hypocrisy is a term that sounds worse than the actuality, and it is a normal part of growing up. An adult who is called a hypocrite has just received a blunt, straightforward criticism. When this same term refers to an adolescent, it does not indicate a character flaw but rather signifies a part of the brain's development. Younger adolescents will often talk or even lecture about a principle that they hold to be true but then totally ignore it in their behavior. For instance, adolescents will talk about a healthy lifestyle while eating fast food, or they will criticize their teachers for global warming and then refuse to carpool to school.

Ignore and tolerate these situations. A suggestion to carpool and eat nutritionally is a good idea (ideally, this is part of the curriculum). A lecture on how they are saying one thing and doing another is probably meaningless until the hardware in their brains catches up with their good intentions.

This illogical attribute diminishes by high school, when we see kids becoming actively involved in their communities. Older adolescents are capable of not only talking the talk but also walking the walk. Build on this new capability by encouraging active involvement in ser-vice projects. At-risk students benefit from required service experi-ences, not just recommended experiences. A spirit of altruism needs to be developed and nurtured. Arrange and mandate opportunities for ser-vice in various school and community settings.

One correctional facility implemented a volunteer project for adolescent males at a retirement home. The boys helped the residents with small chores, played games with them, and periodically worked with them on service projects. One winter and in conjunction with the elderly, the boys knit 300 caps for the needy. The elderly acted as mentors to the boys to teach them how to knit, how to conduct agreeable conversations, and how to exhibit respectable behavior.

Everyone realized that this was a worthy experience for the boys, but the impact on the residents in the retirement home wasn't fully realized until one of the residents who had been particularly interactive with the boys passed away. His widow asked that four of the boys from the correctional facility act as pallbearers, and she thanked them for giving his life meaning. The feeling was mutual.

"NO ONE HAS EVER FELT THE WAY I DO"

Brain changes often make teens believe that they are the first and only ones to experience anything. Whether it's going through a breakup, forgetting a locker combination, or being truant, no one else has ever experienced it. No wonder teens think that adults do not understand them! After all, how could they when their parents and teachers have never felt the way they do?

One mother was trying to comfort her heartbroken daughter after a painful breakup, when the girl looked at her through tear-stained eyes and moaned, "How would you know how I feel? You've never been in love." Rather than countering with the logical and the obvious "What about dad?" Mom chose to show compassion and hold her tongue.

It would be wonderful if there were some magical solution to curb this feeling, but as teachers, we have as our best bet the choice to be aware and then be tolerant. This too will pass.

MORAL DEVELOPMENT

Older teenagers are ready to tackle complex moral dilemmas. They approach problems systematically and realize that two rules might conflict, that things aren't always black and white. Their world is expanding. The teenage brain has the potential to develop morally, but this will not happen without prompting. Teenagers need their space to consider moral issues, and they need opportunities to discuss moral issues with teachers, peers, and parents.

Moral decisions engage many parts of the brain. Long-term memories, emotional memories, visual and auditory memories, and the frontal lobes work in concert for a good moral decision. Consider this dilemma: A good friend wants to cheat on a test, and he wants you to signal the correct answers to him. At least 20 brain structures would apply themselves to this problem. Long-term memories (stored in the cerebral cortex) recall the fun you've had with him, walking the mall, playing video games, and partying, as well as memories of how he's always struggled in school and how he has had to deal with his dad's temper.

Sympathy gets a boost from your visual cortex; the amygdala processes your friend's facial expressions and his embarrassment over his bad grades. The amygdala also brings about a twinge of fear—if you turn him down, what will this do to your friendship, and what about his dad's temper? Your ambivalence activates your premotor cortex, which rehearses slugging him for putting you in this position. At the same time, your frontal lobes keep you calm. The problem-solving function of this structure says that maybe you can make this work, and it suggests that you might just as well help him cheat. At this point, your frontal lobes step in to take command and decide how to kindly yet firmly tell him no.

Moral development doesn't occur automatically; adolescents need to be challenged with various problems, wrestle with a variety of solutions, and sort out their views. The classroom, religious affiliation, and family are all places conducive to encouraging varied views and dynamic discussions in a safe environment. Sensitivity to diversity, sexual harassment, and those with special needs can be developed through education and experiences with diverse populations.

Getting involved in the community is a good way to create awareness of issues and at the same time allow an adolescent to make meaningful contributions to the well-being of others. Ultimately, moral development takes the energy and commitment of action as well as thought. It starts with discussion in the classroom followed by active participation in the community.

SOCIAL SKILLS CLASSES

At-risk students often need direct instruction in social skills. Students need to be able to identify negative comments, actions, and reactions and differentiate them from positive comments, actions, and reactions. Becoming socially and emotionally intelligent increases students' likelihood of remaining in school and improves their ability to get along with peers and teachers. In some schools, this objective becomes a schoolwide project; in others, social skill classes are reserved just for students identified with a special need.

Many memories are stored by events linked to social and emotional situations. Regrettably, when emotions rise to strong levels because of high stress or anger in the classroom, students have difficulty focusing, learning, and remembering information. Creativity and problem solving fly out the window. The emotionally filled amygdala takes over and the reasonably thinking prefrontal cortex takes a snooze.

A social skills curriculum focuses on strategies to help students identify and control their own emotions. Building empathy, fostering confidence, and improving the ability to communicate and cooperate with others are all routinely included in the program. As students learn to strengthen and regulate their social and emotional lives, they do better academically, are more motivated, and get along better with teachers and peers. This ability also aids as a protective factor, helping them resist drugs, pregnancy, gangs, and truancy.

Teaching social skills should not only be taught as a separate class but be integrated into programs addressing other at-risk activities. For instance, drug abuse prevention programs that delve into emotional and social issues of peer pressure, stress, coping skills, decision making, and consequences connected with addiction are usually effective. All the issues contributing to the at-risk behavior need to be addressed.

Strategies commonly used to build social skills:

Storytelling: Tell a personal story about a dilemma that you had during adolescence, or talk about role models such as Rosa Parks and her role in the civil rights movement.
Goal setting: Have students clarify personal goals that are short-term, specific, and attainable.

Group discussion: Discuss a current event that deals with, for example, athletes behaving badly, or problem-solving scenarios, such as that which involves a student who has no one to eat lunch with or who has difficulty in handling a disagreement with a teacher.

Role-playing: Have students practice greeting an adult with proper eye contact, a firm handshake, and suitable speech.

Self-awareness: Discuss different feelings and what produces various emotions in them.

Social skills curriculum topics:

- Listening
- Relating to peers properly
- Recognizing the importance of drug and alcohol prevention
- Setting realistic short-term goals
- Realizing that there are often two sides to an issue
- Recognizing consequences of risky behavior
- Implementing problem-solving strategies
- Utilizing decision-making strategies
- Focusing on the future
- Adjusting to one's physical changes
- Demonstrating sensitivity to others
- Accepting diversity

CHAPTER 5

Emotions Gone Awry

Teenage emotions are flying high and entering the danger zone with no one in the pilot's seat. Teenage behavior can spin out of control in a flash and, once out of control, require Herculean efforts to maneuver a smooth and safe landing.

Did you know that . . .

- males with high testosterone have more aggression?
- violent video games agitate emotional areas of the brain and deter the ability to make thoughtful decisions?
- students with emotional and behavioral disorders have more aggressive and dark thoughts than do their peers?
- adolescents have more negative thoughts in their brains than do adults?

AGGRESSION

Teenagers are naturally drawn to wild and crazy things: "Let's race." "I'm gonna punch your face out." "Sure, I'll try it" (in referring to taking a hit of methadone). They are more impulsive and rash than adults. It comes as no surprise to middle school and high school teachers that of all the emotions, impulse control is the last to develop.

The teenage tendency to take risks comes from a variety of sources, including a desire to impress peers, an indestructible belief about themselves, and the changes in their brain. Novelty and danger are a tantalizing combination. They stimulate dopamine production and create the same rush that drugs such as crack and methadone generate. Add to this a lack of impulse control, and aggressive behavior is spawned.

There appear to be gender differences in regard to aggression, and boys are at greater risk than are girls of displaying it. Research studies have noted male children are six times more likely than female children to be identified as having behavior so aggressive that it disrupts their lives. Aggressive behaviors exhibited by boys in school can be credited to several things, including personal temperament, cultural expectations, learning style, the structure of the classroom, the acceptance of the teacher, and the brain.

The emotional center of the brain, housed in the amygdala, spawns and discharges aggressive behavior. It firmly dominates throughout most of adolescence, even as the logical reasoning area of the brain steadily and optimistically vies for power. By late adolescence, the balance of power changes: The frontal lobes gain influence, and self-regulation improves.

A major stimulant to the amygdala in boys is the male hormone testosterone. Once puberty strikes, boys receive approximately 1,000 times more testosterone than they did as children—about 10 jolts a day. This overstimulates the amygdala (already enlarged in the adolescent boy), which is also associated with aggression and sexual interest. A potentially logical discussion about whose turn it is to present in social studies class can easily explode into an argument. When confronted, boys are perfectly primed to say things like "Why should I have to? Joe doesn't have to."

High testosterone levels can be a blessing, not a curse, if guided in a positive direction. Many professional athletes, prominent businessmen, and famous politicians have elevated levels of testosterone. It is hypothesized that there is a correlation between high testosterone and a competitive nature.

Low levels of serotonin, a calming neurotransmitter, may also be a factor in aggressive behavior. Serotonin is released at a lower rate in teens' brains. Just when teens could use a calming agent, it's in low supply! Interestingly, praise and encouragement come to the rescue because positive social feedback ("Good work!" and "I like how you handled that") from a significant adult (such as a teacher or coach) has been shown to increase serotonin levels in the brain.

Stick to facts during confrontations and try to reduce high emotions. If a teen loses control, stay calm. Adolescents need firm, consistent reactions. When things have cooled down, listen to what teens say and focus on their feelings. Blaming them and accusing them of acting inappropriately is only going to increase their anger and shut down any chances of communication. Discuss appropriate ways to handle an insult or threat. Sometimes, a warning and discussion are all they need, but more often, they need to suffer a consequence, such as writing a letter of apology or serving a detention or in-school suspension. If at all possible, do not make the consequence one of removing the one activity that they love best. That extracurricular activity or friendship may be the one and only thing that helps them control their emotions; without it, they could flounder.

Also be a good role model. Let teens see how you maturely handle the frustration of a computer breakdown or an uncooperative student. People learn by example, and teachers are a huge influence in teenagers' lives. Finally, encourage teens to become involved with extracurricular activities, service clubs, and hobbies. The more supervised a teen is, the less likely he or she is to exhibit inappropriate behaviors. Teenagers who are persistently aggressive may need to attend anger management classes to learn to control their emotions.

Signs of teenage aggression:

- Resisting authority
- Being disrespectful of others
- Relying on aggression to solve problems
- Mediocre academic work (or worse)
- Cutting classes, getting suspended, or dropping out
- Gang involvement
- Alcohol or drug use

BULLIES AND THEIR VICTIMS

Twelve-year-old Tom was actually excited to start middle school. Regrettably, about 2 weeks into school, a boy named Aaron began to bully Tom. Aaron called him names like *girly-boy* and *sissy*. Aaron could tell that the names bothered Tom, which added fuel to the fire. He began to taunt him in front of the other boys: "You're the worst player on the team." "Don't give the ball to him—he'll never make the basket." Then, the "yo mama" jokes started. One day after gym class, Tom returned to his locker and found all his clothes were missing. After searching the area, he found them in the shower room, drenching wet. At this humiliation, he started to cry, only adding fodder to the cruel game.

Teasing and roughhousing can be fun—just ask any middle schooler—but sometimes it crosses the line into bullying. Once the energy shifts and one person is more powerful than another, the fun ends and the bullying begins. Schools are a prime location for bullying; students can't escape the locker room, hallways, or cafeteria. And it takes many forms, such as physical, verbal, and social exclusion.

Bullying often starts in elementary and middle school as a way for the strong to be popular and admired, but ultimately it's all about power. Bullies have a greater-than-average aggressive nature; they want to dominate and control. Once the hitting, slugging, and taunting is over, there is no sense of remorse, nor is responsibility taken for their cruelty. Healthy socioemotional development is not in the cards for them or their victims without adult intervention (over 60% have criminal convictions along with alcoholism and mental health problems as adults).

A great deal of media attention has been given to the subject of bullying, making it easy to believe that it is a constant and continual problem. In reality, the majority of students are never bullied, but for the few who do become victims, anxiety and terror fill their school days. Bullies can often identify their victims a mile away; their insecurities are evident in every step they take. They tend to appear vulnerable, physically weak, and rejected by peers, and they often have overprotective parents.

What you as a teacher can do:

- Intervene if you see bullying (teachers think that they intervene 70% of the time; students say that it is more like 25% of the time).
- Get older peers to serve as monitors for bullying.
- Develop schoolwide rules against bullying.

- Form friendship and support groups for adolescents who are regularly bullied.
- Refer bullies to counselors (they need help).
- Equip students with a line of defense while at the same time not placing responsibility or blame on victims.

What you can advise victims to do:

- Don't believe what the bully says about you.
- Stand up for yourself; give the impression of confidence; don't let bullies know that you're upset; look them in the eye; practice saying "No!" in an assertive manner.
- Watch your body language—don't stoop or hang your head; do take deep breaths.
- Try using humor or a well-chosen word.
- Talk to someone you trust; do not suffer in silence.

In isolation it is impossible for these strategies to work. Students need the support and vigilance of teachers and administrators to combat bullying.

AGGRESSION AND VIOLENT VIDEO GAMES

Researchers have found disturbing evidence concerning teens and violent video games. Video games typically require reflexive reactions, not reflective responses. These games stimulate the amygdala and neutralize the frontal lobes. Teenage boys who engage in excessive violent video play have underactive frontal lobes during the game and long after it has been unplugged. This means that logical, reasonable thinking is muffled and that fast, reactive thinking is stimulated.

This translates into everyday life when the reflective student carefully decides what books and homework they need to gather before leaving for school; estimates an appropriate amount of time to drive, park, and get in the building; and then drives responsibly to school. Teens working on a video-agitated brain find themselves watching television until 10 minutes before school starts and then driving like maniacs through traffic, and they are surprised when they get a costly speeding ticket.

Additionally, violent games trigger testosterone to be released into the system, further agitating the amygdala. Why else would a 15-year-old yell and slam his fist when you interrupt his *Mortal Kombat* computer game?

Neuroscientists and psychologists are pointing to studies that show how media violence arouses aggressive behavior. Violent media messages affect both behavior and empathy. Cutting-edge research shows that violent games make people callous to brutality. After playing violent video games over an extended period in one study, young men showed little reaction to violent crimes, they had become anesthetized by the "virtual" bloodshed.

Teachers do not have control over what video games parents allow or disallow in their homes, but they can make parents and students aware of the dangers. What teachers can do is to help boys learn impulse control (see the chapter 4 section Impulse Control). Teach coping skills, such as exercise; identify trigger words such as *disgusted*, *lazy*, and *stupid*; and encourage age-appropriate ways to handle negative emotions. Praise the proper handling of issues and be generous—everyone needs to hear a good word every now and then.

RECKLESS BEHAVIOR

Ricky and his friends constantly pushed the limits between fun and danger. One evening, Ricky and Troy decided to explore a landfill that was being excavated. Construction workers had left their machinery on-site, and the boys decided to drive the backhoe around the area. Having no experience driving heavy machinery (or machinery of any kind, for that matter), the experience quickly took a tragic turn. Driving down a steep hill, the backhoe went out of control and began to roll. Both boys were thrown from the cab, and Ricky was instantly killed. His younger brother related this story to me. He told me how much he missed his brother and that he still considered him his best friend.

Eighty percent of teens report engaging in one or more risky behaviors during a month. Their transgressions range from the minor to the major: disobeying parents, misbehaving at school, engaging in substance abuse, driving while intoxicated, having unprotected sex, committing theft, and fighting. Why are they doing this? Adolescents are impulsive creatures. Reckless and wild behavior becomes their norm, whereas the knack to plan, monitor, and reflect is put on a back burner. Rising dopamine levels (feeling good) and dwindling serotonin production (a calming agent) add to teens' desire for novel, risky, and extreme adventures.

One study of teen drivers showed that if they were driving alone or with parents, they would stop at a yellow light, an indication of safe driving. If a peer was riding shotgun, they would run the yellow light. Teens thought that this risky business had a positive social impact ("My friend thinks I'm cool") and that it was emotionally arousing ("This is exciting").

When young children get the urge to run across the street, they almost always have an adult (and, ergo, an adult brain) keeping an eye on them, holding their hands, and stopping their motion. Adolescents, in an effort to become independent and self-sufficient (as they should), push that adult away. Too often, they can be seen darting across the proverbial street. Teens need and want monitoring—surrogate frontal lobes—to effectively protect and guide them in their journey to adulthood.

First, as a teacher, adjust your expectations and realize that teens will take risks. Next, monitor and prohibit risky and dangerous behavior in the classroom. Set clear limits and enforce consequences fairly. In science class, mandate appropriate safety skills; in physical education, require that equipment be used in an appropriate manner.

Encourage extracurricular activities. Keep teens active in positive programs that are meaningful to them. Support middle school after-school programs in your community because supervision translates into safety. In my community, young juvenile crime decreased by 42% the first year that our middle school after-school programs started. The local police force directly attributed the reduction to the after-school program.

FIGHTING

Fighting in school can erupt quickly and explode out of control in a nanosecond. The very same brain structures and functions that put students at risk for aggression, anger, and reckless behavior also put students at risk for fighting.

During seventh period at a local high school, everyone was in the halls ready to head home. Two boys approached each other in an apparently ordinary meeting, when suddenly one boy slammed the other into the lockers and a full-blown fight erupted before everyone's eyes. Students often break up fights within seconds, devoid of teachers even being aware that they started, but these boys were not in the mood to listen to any student warnings. Teachers broke the fight up, and both boys were taken to detention. The reason for the fight? One boy had been told that the other boy had stolen his mother's jewelry. He had made no effort to confirm the allegations (a week later, the real robber was found), nor had he contacted authorities. Instead, he flew out of control. Emotions trumped logic.

Be proactive and look out for possible trouble between students. If you believe that students are nearing the boiling point, intervene and talk to them before they get there. Do not allow bullying in your class; it's just a precursor to a fight. Discuss the school policy and your own views on bullying, and then follow through if you observe it. Bullying often occurs outside the classroom, in the hallways, cafeteria, and parking lot, which is sufficient reason for adult supervision in those student-ruled areas. Encourage positive behavior.

Once a fight starts, do your best not to leave the area. First, try to stop the fight with a verbal command, and instruct a student to go for help. Be firm and clear as you direct the students watching the fight to leave the area, because their safety is of primary concern. After the fight has been broken up, remove the individuals involved from the classroom or school area and take them to the principal's or counselor's office. Document the event while it's fresh in your mind.

It may be a good idea to discuss the fight with your class at some time; however, when emotions are running high, return to your normal lesson plans or assign a quiet activity such as silent reading. Engaging students in a discussion at this juncture may result in another fight breaking out. A discussion should wait for cooler and calmer heads.

EMOTIONALLY AND BEHAVIORALLY DISTURBED STUDENTS

"That black magic marker is mine."

"Screw you."

"You f—head, give it to me."

This is an excerpt from a "conversation" overheard in a classroom for emotionally and behaviorally disturbed (EBD) high school students as they worked on a poster project that went out of control. EBD students will fight about anything, anytime, anywhere.

Behaviors exhibited by EBD students include a laundry list of negative actions: lack of personal relationships (with peers, teachers, and family), aggression, mood swings, anxieties, confusion, learning problems, depression, and oppositional behavior. EBD students are on an individualized education plan, which ensures that they receive proper educational, behavioral, and medical support.

Four areas of the brain play a role in emotional and behavioral disorders: the basal ganglia, the prefrontal cortex, the temporal lobes, and the cingulate system. All of these areas of the brain work against the EBD student in controlling emotions and behaviors.

One of the responsibilities of the basal ganglia is to regulate the brain's anxiety levels. An overactive basal ganglia can create anxieties that foster serious emotional problems, such as shutting down, extreme shyness, and low or high motivation. When facing age-appropriate situations, these students find that they lack the ability to cope.

The prefrontal cortex helps people make decisions, use good judgment, and control aggression. A dysfunctional prefrontal cortex may result in behaviors such as impulsivity, aggression, and violence.

The temporal lobes play an important role in emotion and behaviors. Dysfunctional temporal lobes produce behavioral characteristics such as paranoia, violent behavior (provoked and unprovoked), irritability, and dark thoughts.

The cingulate system assists in changing attention from one task to another. EBD students have an increased level of activity in their cingulate systems, and they are controlled by their own negative thoughts and their perceptions of others' thoughts. This makes it difficult for them to transition between activities and it often results in argumentative and oppositional behavior.

To assist EBD students, develop a school climate that ensures safety and has high expectations. A firm foundation of consistency and routine benefits the emotional control needed by the EBD student. Stating and posting rules is enough for most students, but EBD students benefit from a multiple-intelligences approach to learning rules. For instance, physically practicing, role-playing, and drawing pictures of rules will enhance their ability to follow the rules.

EBD students often suffer from low-self esteem; they are not able to meet their teachers', parents', or society's expectations on a daily basis. Short-term attainable goals will enhance their ability to achieve academically and see their progress before their frustration levels peak. Social skills need to be both directly and indirectly taught throughout the day.

EBD students often blow up and are willing to argue over the minutest issue. Behavior management plans work well in the EBD classroom or separate site. A structure of rewards for good behavior and consequences for bad behavior helps rewire the EBD brain. Do not argue with these students, but at the same time don't ignore inappropriate behavior. As the adult, you are the role model, so stay calm and be consistent.

DEPRESSION

Reports of feeling very happy drop during the teen years. Adolescents have a relatively negative spirit until about age 18. Before that time, they face more emotional turmoil and have a difficult time looking at life positively. Although a subpositive disposition is the norm for most teenagers, in some, it hits serious levels and depression sets in.

A high percentage of at-risk teens suffer from clinical depression. Depression is thought to be a combination of genetics, environment, and biology. Triggering and sustaining depression in an adolescent may run the gamut from sexual abuse and bad grades to breaking up with a boyfriend or girlfriend. What is viewed by adults as a normal part of growing up can seem like the end of the world for a teenager and thus lead to a serious depression. Unfortunately, the at-risk teen is often dealing with the natural ups and downs of teenage life along with more serious and troubling social issues.

Puberty also bears a part in teenage depression. As a person moves through puberty, the possibility of his or her suffering from depression escalates. In fact, progression through puberty is a more accurate predictor of depression onset than chronological age is. Progesterone puts girls at an even higher risk. Once progesterone is released into the system, it allows cortisol, the stress hormone, to run rampant, which makes it difficult for girls to restore their mental harmony.

Lower levels of serotonin during adolescence also add to feelings of depression. Normally, serotonin inhibits the firing of neurons and makes us feel calm, relaxed, and peaceful. The soothing neurotransmitter works as a check and balance with the emotional amygdala. The majority of teens suffer no negative consequences with low serotonin levels, but for some teens, it seems to increase the likelihood of depression. Researchers offer two theories for why this happens. Some speculate that certain teenage brains are unable to properly use serotonin, whereas others hypothesize that the levels are so low that they are unable to act as a calming agent.

The right prefrontal cortex, which controls negative emotions, is the part of the brain that is in control in depressed people. This permits gloomy thoughts and dark memories to overshadow all other thoughts. Much like an annoying jingle that you can't get out of your head, bad messages ("I'm stupid, I'm stupid, I'm stupid") run over and over through depressed people's minds, sinking them further into despair. Other parts of the brain are also negatively affected. The hippocampus shrinks in size with chronic depression, and with severe depression its neurons begin to wither and die, which makes it difficult to remember old information (such as happier times) and new information (such as homework assignments).

Depression affects the hippocampus, the part of the brain in charge of short-term memories. As the student becomes more depressed, he or she will have more and more difficulty remembering information. A lesson about acute angles learned one day will be forgotten by the next.

As a teacher, you need to understand adolescent depression and be on the lookout for it. If you believe that a student is depressed, intervene. Talk to the student; make a referral to the school counselor or nurse; and otherwise enlarge his or her support circle. If a student wants to confide in you, listen, but know your limits and stick to your boundaries in the role of teacher.

SUICIDE

Derek was seventeen. By all accounts, he was the brightest boy in the school, but he was deeply troubled. He wore a long dark trench coat to school the day after Columbine, was immersed in dark thoughts, and loved the thought of intimidating others.

One day, he was talking to a teacher about his next-semester courses when he went off on a tangent and said, "My dad probably wouldn't care if I wasn't around, but my mom would be sad." Without missing a beat, he reconvened the conversation on scheduling classes for next semester.

After the conference, the teacher spoke with the school counselor and recounted the disturbing conversation. The counselor assured her that it was nothing to be concerned about, but the conversation haunted him. He knew that Derek's uncle had committed suicide a year ago. He made a phone call to Derek's social worker. She was unaware of any thoughts of suicide but knew that Derek had given away some of his CDs and a special jacket to friends. The pieces of the puzzle suddenly fit together, and an immediate intervention was done. As feared, Derek was contemplating suicide, and professional help was sought.

The belief that you can't stop someone who really wants to commit suicide is a myth. Most people are ambivalent about this final decision. If you are suspicious that a student is contemplating suicide, be proactive.

Adolescents that are experiencing depression, low self-esteem, and anxiety are at added risk of suicide. Tragically, it is the second-leading cause of teenage death, surpassed only by automobile accidents. Between the ages of 14 and 25, there is a dramatic increase in suicide rates.

Signs to watch for in teens that might be suicidal:

- Talking about suicide or death in general
- A preoccupation with morbid subject matter
- Talking about going away
- Giving away personal possessions
- Talking about feeling hopeless or guilty
- Withdrawing from friends and family
- Losing the desire to go out or take part in favorite activities
- Having trouble concentrating or thinking clearly
- Experiencing changes in eating, cleanliness, or sleeping habits
- Weight loss
- Engaging in self-destructive behavior (drinking alcohol, taking drugs, self-cutting)
- Poor school performance
- Depression
- Suffering a loss, such as a death in the family, a divorce, or a breakup
- Sudden outbursts of temper
- Expressing a plan for suicide

What should teachers do?

- Take warning signs seriously.
- Don't devalue feelings by saying that everything is okay.
- Communicate that you care and are listening.
- Be nonjudgmental.
- Directly ask teens hinting at suicide if they are planning to hurt themselves.
- Do not promise to keep conversations about suicidal intentions a secret.
- Seek professional help.
- If at all possible, do not leave a suicidal teenager alone.

If a suicide occurs, send cards to the family and the student's best friends, offering support; everyone touched needs a compassionate word and thought. Speak with the school counselor and other teachers about any related concerns. Allow students to discuss it with their peers; they need time to make sense of something that just doesn't make sense. Watch for delayed reactions; it may appear that students are adjusting, but weeks later, they can have a breakdown as a delayed reaction to the tragedy.

CHAPTER 6

The Social Lives of Teens

One minute, teens scream and insist that they be allowed to dye their hair Kool-Aid red to truly express themselves; the next, they are crying because they don't own the same jeans as everybody else. Blending conformity and individuality in looks, thoughts, and activities creates a mix that needs a teenage brain to sort out.

Did you know that . . .

- girls, compared to boys, have increased ability in the parts of the brain that help them socialize?
- peer pressure is greatest during ninth grade?
- conforming with peers helps validate teenagers?
- teens fine-tune their negotiating and problem-solving skills by hanging and talking with friends?
- the brain really does feel great when in love?

FRIENDS

Marta was a bright girl, a troubled girl, a teenage girl with few sources of support in her life. She was promiscuous, drank too much, and experimented with drugs. By age 16, she was attending an alternative school because of the continual problems that she had at the regular high school. All that aside, Marta had potential. You could see it in her eyes and hear it in her voice. She could make something of herself if she would just get her act together.

Unfortunately, during her tenure at the alternative school, she got into a verbal fight with a policeman that resulted in her taking a swing at him.

Subsequently, she was sent to a juvenile detention center for 30 days—a long time by anyone's account. When she returned to school, something was different about Marta. She had made a conscious choice about her future. She wanted to get on track, and she never wanted to go back to the detention center. When things in her life got a little dicey and she became faced with the possibility of a return visit, she would calm down, rethink her actions, and control herself. She was making progress.

In one of my many discussions with her, we talked about her friends and how they kept dragging her down into dark and murky waters. This was where conversation and progress stopped for Marta. She refused to even discuss giving up any of her friendships, and the ultimate cost she paid was high. For every step forward that she took, they relentlessly pulled her back two. Still, she considered them her emotional network, and in her mind, discarding them was not an option.

The at-risk teen needs the same things that other teens do from friendship—plus some. Friends play an especially important role in the lives of teens who feel a lack of support at home. Their belief that their parents don't understand them, the lack of monitoring at home ("It's ten o'clock. Where are you?"), and the general neglect that they experience push them toward their peers. Understandably, there are potential problems when peer influence outweighs parental influence. Normally, peer groups tend to stress the wild and wooly side of life; partying is given a high priority. In moderation, this is typical, even desirable; but if there isn't an accompanying adult message, juggling revelry with responsibilities becomes a shaky proposition.

Girls have a distinct advantage on the social scene. The hippocampus, the part of the brain associated with transferring short-term memory into long-term memory, is particularly large in girls. Neuroscientists speculate that this helps girls as they network and navigate cliques and crowds. (Finally, their brains are developing a skill they value—the ability to party!)

Through academic and social experiences, the teenage brain matures, and with this, teens have the desire to form intimate relationships. They want to share private conversation with a close friend, but they are in the process of figuring out what to tell and to whom to tell it. With time, they recognize that not everyone needs to be privy to their deepest and darkest secrets.

Sharing confidential tidbits with the right friend is a full-time job for most teens. They see each other all day in school, are on the cell phone in the car, and immediately instant-message each other upon arrival at home. There is an upside to the constant flow of conversation—that is, if it doesn't hamper schoolwork: It helps validate teenagers, and it assures them that their thoughts and actions are in the norm.

Friendships provide more than someone to talk to; friends instigate and plunge into fun together. Let the dopamine flow! Teens are attracted to novelty, and their peers supply this in abundance. Get a group of teens together, and the good times roll. Teens, like adults and older children, gravitate to people who enjoy similar activities and understand their thoughts and interests. "We're all into cars." "He loves the *Guitar Hero* computer game, and so do I." "We like the same music and the same TV shows—we like reality TV shows and rap and hip-hop—a big mixture."

Loyalty is one of the most valued elements of friendship; it acts as a protective shield to the brain, ensuring a line of defense against the threat of being alone, teased, or tormented. Teens look for someone they can count on through the good times and the bad. The meaning of loyalty and commitment can be seen in comments such as "My friends mean everything to me; I know I can always count on them" and "I can talk to her about anything; she always understands."

It's important as a teacher to foster positive friendships; at-risk friends tend to have other at-risk friends, leading to at-risk activities. In the classroom, put students into heterogeneous small groups; encourage them to participate in extracurricular activities; and give them a chance to explore a variety of interests. Such activities cultivate a safe space where students get to know themselves and their peers. Discussions that spark a variety of viewpoints scan new ideas onto the at-risk students' radar screens and set the stage for sensitivity and perspective taking.

Common activities outside of school for teens:

- Hanging with friends
- Watching television
- Playing computer games
- Cruising in a car

- Shopping at the mall
- Talking on the phone
- Logging onto MySpace and Facebook
- Drinking alcohol

TECHNO FRIENDSHIPS

Seventeen-year-old Jeanie shared a story about one of her best friends, Libby. Libby seemed happy and well adjusted, but underneath she had self-esteem issues. Her friends thought that she had a lot going for her: She was an honor student, had a beautiful voice, and was surrounded by a loyal group of friends.

Midway through her senior year, she stopped going out with friends and stopped going to chorus class. She was uncommunicative and wouldn't give any of her friends an explanation for her change in behavior. This was out of character for Libby. Jeanie decided to take some initiative and call Libby's mom. When she told Libby's mom the situation, her mother was shocked—she had no idea that any of this was going on. Libby's mom wanted some answers, so she called the school and found out that Libby had indeed dropped chorus. Further investigation into the situation found that Libby had hooked up with a 40-year-old over the Internet. It didn't make sense to anyone. As Jeanie said, "Libby's the last person that I thought would get mixed up with somebody on the Internet."

The age of computers has put a new face on friendship. Girls and boys alike are turning to the websites MySpace and Facebook to create personal profiles, exhibit photos, and communicate with online friends. Evidence suggests that such sites represent a mix of positive and negative influence. There is no doubt that these Internet sites are popular and that they are certainly the wave of the future. On one hand, they provide 24-hour contact and support for teenagers. On the other, teens exercise a lack of discretion when they post on their sites and unwittingly invite Internet predators to get to know them.

Particularly problematic are chat rooms. Lonely, naïve kids e-mail and chat with strangers, believing them to be friends who are always available and understanding to them. Cyberstalkers prey on immature and forlorn kids. Too many adolescents have been talked into face-to-face meetings. The news periodically reports incidents of 12- and 13-year-olds being lured to board buses and travel to distant hotels to meet their "special friends." Teenagers need to become as savvy with the message as they are with the medium.

PEER PRESSURE

Alison was 16, likeable, and fun-loving. She lived in a small town near a river surrounded by bluffs. One day, she and a group of friends were messing around by the river. The girls were spending their time chatting and flirting with the boys, and the boys were jumping off the bluffs into the river—a dangerous but thrilling sport. At the insistence of her friends, Alison felt pressure to join in the boy's fun. Nervously, she made a run for the bluff but at the last moment chickened out. She tried to stop her forward motion, but unfortunately, it was too late. She fell approximately 50 feet onto a rocky overhang. She broke both of her feet, and it took a rescue squad more than 2 hours to rescue her.

Peer pressure. The very phrase sends visions of wild parties, dare-devil driving, and sexual experimentation flashing before adults' eyes. But to teenagers, peers are priceless. They represent fun and acceptance.

Peers are critical to the development of teenage identity and self-esteem. Self-esteem is developed through interactions both emotional ("I feel good, proud, satisfied with myself") and cognitive ("I got an A on the math test; I gave a great answer in government class"). The limbic areas (in charge of emotions) and the prefrontal cortex (in charge of reasonable thought) converge to form beliefs about how one views, accepts, and respects oneself.

Ninth grade tends to be a pivotal year regarding peer groups. The friends that teens make, their commitment to school, and the activities they join set the tone for their remaining high school years. The right peer group can create a net of activities and fun that either shield teens from at-risk behavior such as drugs and alcohol, dropping out of school, and promiscuity or compound problems by presenting at-risk behavior as something normal and expected.

Teens will risk detention, suspension, and losing a teacher's trust to identify with and be accepted by a group. Once negatively influenced, they slide easily downhill. Peer pressure gone too far may result in delinquency, alcohol abuse, and promiscuity. Research has found a stronger correlation between peer influence and student alcohol use than between parental influence and drinking.

Middle school after-school programs are one way to ensure supervision of young adolescents while they interact with their peers. These programs provide teens a wonderful social experience in a safe environment. Choice is usually a part of these programs; teens can choose from sports, dance, art, and computer games as ways to spend their late afternoons. A teen's peers definitely affect the choices that a teen makes in these programs, but the choices are healthy, and the adult monitors serve as a protective factor against negative peer pressure. Unfortunately, money for these programs is being reduced, and many programs are being eliminated around the country.

CONFORMITY

Do you go to extremes to own the right jacket and the right tennis shoes? Do you actually try to dress like your friends? Have you been known to quickly switch the radio station so that your friends won't know that you are listening to country music? Would you ever eat at McDonald's even though you prefer a homemade salad? If you answered "yes" to any or all of these questions, you are probably a teenager.

Adolescence is a time of monumental angst, uncertainty, and self-consciousness. One of the best antidotes to these trials and tribulations is conforming to one's peer group. Conforming plays a special role in soothing teen insecurity. Wearing the right jeans, listening to the cool music, and, in general, looking and thinking like peers assure teens that they are okay and accepted. Teenagers are attempting to create the perfect blend of individuality and acceptance.

Crowds and cliques take on their own personalities, each with its own distinct similarities. One minute, everyone in the group is wearing baggy jeans and listening to P. Diddy, and the next, they are all in cropped pants with belly-button rings. Conformity helps them establish their identities as they decide "Yes, this is me" or "No, this is not me. I better try something else." As Marybeth said excitedly, "My friends and I always text-message each other to find out what we're going to wear; sometimes we all wear the same top. Jana got her nose pierced; she looks good. I plan to do the same, just not for a while."

Conformity is a route to popularity, and teen magazines, television shows, and models are supplying the roadmap. Brand consciousness seems to increase during the teenage years. Teens rely on brands to project a positive image to others and to bolster their own self-confidence. Teens suffering from low self-esteem are especially captivated by brand names.

If possible, support teens' conformity needs. Make no comments when students dress like their peers, talk like their peers, and follow their peers like sheep (as long as they are in the vicinity of reasonable behavior). These actions are an important part of confirming who they are. Overlook their choices, even when teens appear with burgundy highlights in their hair and dog collars around their necks. Every generation has its own music, a look that is all its own, and a vocabulary that sets it apart; so, don't expect anything less from this generation. (It's almost a rite of passage to shock the older generation and garner its disdain—every generation does it.) Do be aware, however, of the media's message to teens in relation to conformity. Not measuring up to the perfect body leads to a negative identity and low self-esteem (see the chapter 7 section Eating Disorders).

HANGIN' AND TALKIN'

Just *hangin'* and *talkin'* is healthy teenage behavior and actually has an important purpose in an adolescent's development. As teachers, we tend to witness this in the lunchroom or during after-school activities. Teenagers learn to make decisions and problem-solve by thrashing and mulling over various whims and urges: Brainstorming, reflecting, and proposing are all part of the process. This is time-intensive work for the teenager. Sometimes, we watch and wonder as a group of teens spend a whole lunch period just discussing what they are going to do. At the end of lunch, they leave for their next classes with the discussion as the only part of the activity accomplished. At first glance, it seems like they have wasted their time, but they are actually preparing their brain to take on the adult responsibilities of planning, negotiating, and decision making.

Resist the temptation to suggest activities. Trust me — no one will listen. A teacher who kept interjecting opinions was amazed at how none of his helpful ideas were followed or even appreciated. Teachers need to realize that finding consensus is an important skill to develop and take into the adult world. What seems like time being wasted is actually time well spent in developing the teen brain. Leave teens alone and let their minds ramble.

DATING, LOVE, AND BREAKUPS

"We had a huge catfight on campus this year. One girl's boyfriend dumped her, and another girl gave him a ride to the football game. It was totally innocent; he just said, 'I need a ride,' and so she gave him one. His ex-girlfriend just lost it and started chasing her around school the next day — she wanted to fight her. A teacher got punched. She was so angry that it didn't matter that teachers were trying to hold her back. One of the basketball coaches was a big man, and he had trouble holding her. The secretary hid the other girl in the kitchen cooler. I couldn't believe it." As they say, hell hath no fury like a woman scorned. Falling in love, dating, and breaking up are all part of the adolescent dream and nightmare.

Adolescence is an appropriate time to learn about the opposite sex. Estrogen sashays down the school hallways, and testosterone thunders toward her. Puberty has ambushed the sexually dormant child. Never will teens more easily learn how to get along and do the mating dance than at this time — it is one of those windows of opportunity.

Love is as much a matter of the brain as it is the heart. During fMRI scans, regions of the brain actually light up when pictures of one's girlfriend or boyfriend are shown. Not surprisingly, these parts of the brain are all linked with feeling good and having pleasant urges. Love releases a generous dose of feel-good enhancers — dopamine peaks and oxytocin streams — that stirs up feelings of desire and affection. Girls experience particularly elevated levels of oxytocin, preparing them to nurture and cuddle. When this biochemical concoction converges on the brain, adolescents are vulnerable to bouts of intense adoration.

The teen brain stays in love for about 4 months; for adults, this time is expanded to 18 to 24 months (at last, an adult advantage). This partially explains the short-term relationships that teens engage in. One minute, a girl can't get Adam off her mind, and the next, she is dancing with Paul. Young teens often daydream about liking a person to whom they've never or rarely spoken. Older adolescents are more cautious in whom they refer to as their boyfriend or girlfriend. It is only after the hot and heavy 4-month period that the logical part of the brain is called on to assess the pros and cons of a relationship.

It is important to realize that a preoccupation with the opposite sex (one bordering on obsession) is normal; be tolerant but vigilant. Monitoring is vital. The sexual tension between teens as they head to class is almost tangible, so ensure that adult supervision is in place and arrange directed activities as protective shields against irresponsible behavior. Too much free time leads to risky business.

In middle school, breakups are fairly routine and, for the most part, taken in stride. Breakups are much more traumatic in high school. You will see a girl weeping in the hall or a boy flooding his body with alcohol after a bad breakup. Teenage relationship needs are complex, and their coping skills are underdeveloped, which leaves them lacking ways to appropriately soothe their pain. Breaking up is one of the most common causes of adolescent depression, suicide, and murder. Additionally, because their identities are not fully formed, a breakup makes teens question who they are in a negative way.

Do not underestimate a teenager's pain. Don't be surprised if they slow down academically while they heal. It's common to go through a mini-depression after a breakup; this includes a loss of energy and a desire to sleep. One high school teacher consciously ignored a girl for one class period while she laid her head on her desk, too sad after a breakup to participate in class. You may see grades fall and students withdraw in the classroom. Teachers and schools offer routine and consistency in these sensitive times. It's not the school's role to intervene in these matters, but teachers do need to be on the look out for depression and suicide.

CHAPTER 7

Getting Physical

Puberty 101: "Am I doing it correctly?" This question is so frequently asked during adolescence that it should be a required class. Young adolescents are undergoing changes of body, mind, and spirit. Understanding the cognitive and emotional connections to the physical changes offers teachers a head start in dealing with the pubescent teen.

Did you know that . . .

- puberty starts in the brain?
- the area of the brain associated with pleasure and pain is larger and denser in heterosexual males than in homosexual males?
- long-term anorexia and bulimia cause a loss of brain matter?
- steroids activate aggressive areas of the brain?
- the teenager brain receives the message to sleep at a time different from that in child and adult brains?

PUBERTY

A group of eighth-grade girls confided that the worst thing about becoming a woman was gym class. Their school had public showers available after gym and a special private shower for girls having their periods. When pressed to remember, the group of girls could think of only one girl who had ever used the private shower throughout middle school. As one girl put it, "I couldn't decide if it was worse to shower in public or let people know I was having my period."

Against conventional wisdom, puberty starts with the brain, not the body. The hypothalamus—the part of the brain responsible for pain, pleasure, and sexual interest—begins revving its engine around age 11 for girls and age 13 for boys. Estrogen and testosterone wash over the brain, and everything begins to change in seemingly random ways: whiskers, breasts, menstrual periods, wet dreams, and getting taller and lankier by the minute. The rapid growth and wide variation between individuals make teens hypersensitive to their appearance. There are late bloomers and early bloomers, and nobody feels like a just-right bloomer. At no other time is self-esteem so closely connected to body image. Normally, body image shapes about 25% of self-esteem, but during the teen years, it can wreak havoc on teens' feelings of self-worth.

As teachers, our goal is to help adolescents adjust to their new bodies. Talk to teens about what's happening physically. Research shows that boys and girls who are knowledgeable about puberty have an easier transition through it. Never tease a student about physical looks.

The next thing that we can do to help teens adjust to puberty is to take their focus off their bodies. Compliment them on something besides their looks. It's amazing how many compliments are given strictly on a person's hair, face, or clothing. Spotlighting something besides looks is healthy for all teens. This is a particularly important strategy for teens with eating disorders, in whom body image consumes their thoughts.

Keep them engaged in things they liked as children. If they liked sports, encourage them to stay in sports; if they liked singing, encourage that. Girls in particular lose their childhood interests and become overly interested in what the media tells them is important (like becoming sexual objects). Participation in activities can be an antidote to the media's message. And don't jump to conclusions about what is going through their heads. Teens' being interested in sex and their bodies is normal and should not be interpreted as being sexually active.

Because teens are beginning to move outside the family, this is a perfect time to get them involved in the community and nonprofit organizations. Volunteering is a powerful tool for taking the focus off of themselves and reestablishing it on people who can benefit from their help. Volunteers do meaningful work that reinforces the adolescents' positive self-image. Encourage teens to form multigenerational relationships; it helps reinforce a healthy perspective of life. Community service can run the gamut from enlisting in a highly structured national organization, such as a blood bank, to visiting the local nursing home.

SEXUALITY

Sex on the school bus, in the school bathroom, under the bleachers— what are they thinking? Although out of the ordinary, these are all documented incidents.

Male teachers speak of their frustration when girls come to school with tops that reveal tummies and cleavage, clearly rebelling against school policy. When confronted with "You need to go to the office because your clothes are inappropriate," the girls quickly, smugly, and with attitude respond by saying, "Why? What are you looking at?" Make no mistake about it; they know that this makes the male teachers uncomfortable. Teenage mission accomplished.

About half of all high school graduates have had sex. Rates are higher for males, minorities, and students from lower socioeconomic groups. The following factors put them at risk for sexual activity: living in a single-parent home; having an older sister who is sexually active or who has a baby; the belief that peers are sexually active; being an early bloomer in puberty; and hanging out with peers who drink, use drugs, are delinquent, or are promiscuous. The consequences of engaging in sex during adolescence are physical and emotional and include contracting STDs, pregnancy, low self-esteem, and a negative identity.

The onset of puberty and a teenager's tendency to fall in love (see chapter 6 section Dating, Love, and Breakups) increase the chances of sexual exploration. Researchers have theorized that sexual identity and physical attraction are hardwired into the brain before birth—sexuality is a state of mind. Teen brains may put adolescents at risk for wanting to engage in sex, but a sex-saturated media and a lack of adult supervision are the reasons that teenagers actually engage in it.

Parents' working long hours, parents' having addictions, and the reduction in after-school programs have left teenagers to fend for themselves. These teens tend to have a cynical view of the future, which further puts them at risk for promiscuity. Adolescent boys try to define their manhood by the number of their sexual conquests, some going so far as to create gangs that keep score. Promiscuity is not just a sexual issue; it is usually a red flag of low self-esteem, defiance, or abuse. These underlying issues must be addressed if a teen is to receive meaningful help.

Fortunately, teenage pregnancy rates are on the decline, but if a girl does become pregnant, she's going to need all the help she can get from family, friends, and teachers. Teen mothers are ill-prepared to face the responsibilities of raising a child—it really is a case of babies raising babies. Rosa was a pleasant 17-year-old girl who got pregnant, had a baby boy, and decided to raise him on her own. Social services personnel were aware that her family was pretty much nonexistent, and they were on the alert to periodically check up with her.

Rosa moved into a trailer with a middle-aged woman who sincerely wanted to help Rosa and the baby. Unfortunately, neither Rosa nor the woman she looked to as a mentor knew anything about infants. Two weeks after giving birth, social services made a visit to the trailer and found that Rosa had been giving the baby 7-Up for the first 2 weeks of his life. The woman had suggested that it would help calm the baby's tummy when he cried. And so the cycle begins—at-risk moms raising at-risk babies.

A mother's education is the strongest indicator that her children will complete high school. The better educated the mother, the more likely that her children will remain in school. School districts that provide day care and flexible schedules for teen moms are investing in the future.

With all the sexual innuendo and overt references on television, in music, and in society in general, you'd think we'd all be comfortable educating our students about sex, but we're not. A school's first line of defense is a comprehensive age-appropriate sex education program. The debate about doing so is now over: 93% of Americans believe that sex education should be taught in school. Programs that focus on good decision making seem to make the most difference. As it should be, individual school districts have been put in charge of making decisions on what curriculum best meets the needs of the students in their communities.

GAYS AND LESBIANS

Naomi was outgoing, willful, athletic, from a strong Catholic family, and gay. She came out to her friends and parents in 10th grade. Her parents' reaction was disapproving and unyielding. Naomi woke up the morning after coming out and was told that she would no longer be attending public high school but would instead be enrolling in a private Catholic school. She felt abandoned. There was no discussion, and the change of schools seemed like a punishment.

A week later, she slit her wrists. Fortunately, she was found in time and thus hospitalized. But acceptance was not in the cards for Naomi. While in the hospital, her father and siblings were compassionate and worried about her, but her mother simply said, "You know you're going to hell." Peace of mind eventually came to Naomi, but it was not an easy journey. Parents who deny homosexuality and are unsupportive become contributing factors in the cases of half of all runaways, one third of suicides, and a significant amount of alcohol and drug abuse.

Brain differences have been found between gay and straight males. The hypothalamus—as mentioned, the part of the brain in charge of pain, pleasure, thirst, hunger, and sexual drive—is found to be smaller and thinner in gay males. It is similar in size to heterosexual females (as opposed to the larger and thicker hypothalamus found in heterosexual males). To date, no brain differences have been found with lesbians, although the gay female body has its own physical differences. For example, the inner ear of gay females is configured differently from that of straight females, and their fingerprints have a different number of points.

If a gay teen needs support, teachers can help connect him or her with a support group or counselor. If a student comes out to you, realize that he or she has probably spent many hours preparing for this conversation and is very nervous. Growing up in a community that may not approve of gay lifestyles makes it impossible for such a teen to predict how this news will be received.

Remember that the student has not changed; he or she is the same person that you've had in class all year. Just be a good listener. If you find yourself too shocked or too negative to have a conversation, say that you need time to digest this news, and set a time for further discussion. It's better to delay the talk than it is to say something that you will later regret.

Common questions to ask:

- "How long have you known that you are gay?"
- "Has it been hard to carry this secret?"
- "What can I do to help?"

TRANSGENDER

Billy was 15, wore a bra and panties, enjoyed applying makeup, and spent a great deal of time making sure that his hair was done just right. Billy would be the first to tell you that he was a woman trapped in a man's body. Physically, Billy had the body of a male, but emotionally and mentally, he was a female.

Neuroscientists have found strong evidence that male transsexuals have significantly smaller hypothalamus than do their heterosexual counterparts. Researchers speculate that gender identity is a result of the interactions between the developing brain and sex hormones. They believe that this is the tip of the iceberg in transgender brain differences.

Not surprisingly puberty is often a nightmare for these students. Many face depression and other emotional disturbances as they attempt to define their identities. Reactions, adjustments, and acceptance for who they are run the full gamut, from healthy acceptance to self-loathing. Teachers can help by being tolerant and accepting of their dress, behavior, and interests.

Tips for dealing with transgender students:

- Use the name and the pronoun that the student prefers (if you misspeak, apologize).
- Provide private restrooms.
- Arrange appropriate locker rooms for physical education.
- Respect transgender teens' privacy; keep biological gender confidential, if they desire.

- Respect their clothing choices; if possible, make accommodations in school policy.
- Refer them to a counselor or other professional, if needed.
- Suggest transgender support groups.
- Protect them from harassment; forbid it in school.

EATING DISORDERS

Eating habits are usually established during the childhood years, strayed from during adolescence, and returned to during adulthood. In the normal-weight teen, nutrients first go to vital organs, such as the heart and kidneys, then to bones and muscle for musculoskeletal growth, and finally, to cognition. About half of teens eat five times a day, which can actually be a healthy routine if they eat nutritious foods. Blueberries, beans, broccoli, oats, oranges, pumpkin, salmon, soy, spinach, tea, tomatoes, turkey, walnuts, and yogurt are all considered healthy brain food.

Eating has become much more of an issue during the last decade, with unrealistic media expectations of body image and a rise in eating disorders such as obesity, anorexia, and bulimia. Compounding the problem is readily available fast food, larger portions, and an increase in sedentary activities such as watching television and playing on the computer. No one suffers from this trend more than the adolescent; eating disorders generally originate in the teen years.

The brain plays a role in eating disorders. Obesity has been linked to leptin, a neurotransmitter that notifies the brain that the stomach is full. In all likelihood, teenagers who are obese are not properly receiving the leptin message. Without this message, they continue to eat more and more. Furthermore, an obese person's brain tends to have fewer dopamine receptors. Dopamine is released after a satisfying meal, which is why a plate of chicken alfredo or chocolate cake leaves one feeling so satisfied. This feeling does not register with obese people until they have gorged themselves, which leads to further weight gain.

Although anorexia and bulimia have primarily cultural origins, the brain plays a small role in these disorders. Some sufferers of anorexia and bulimia have elevated levels of serotonin, a chemical in the brain that helps regulate moods and behaviors. The compulsion that one feels toward food—that is, to eat or not eat—is aggravated by the malfunctioning of calming agents in the brain and the fact that this tends to increase compulsive behavior. Over an extended period, anorexia and bulimia cause a loss of brain matter, putting in jeopardy the quality of all decisions that sufferers make, including those concerning food.

Schools can help by providing healthy snacks and meals, along with vending machines that don't stock sugary items and soda. Eliminate the fast-food options from the cafeteria. Educating students on nutrition and healthy living is an important part of the curriculum.

Suggestions for combating eating disorders:

- Don't constantly talk about weight or emphasize diets.
- Encourage interests and activities. Hobbies and skills enhance self-esteem and act as a protective factor.
- Talk about magazine photos and the techniques used to achieve unrealistic representations, such as airbrushing.
- Include nutrition in the curriculum.
- Recommend professional help when required—recovery is possible.
- In talking to teens, coaches and physical education teachers should choose criticisms carefully because they are particularly influential in how adolescents view their bodies.
- Support physical education requirements in your school.
- Do not encourage weight loss in sports such as wrestling, gymnastics, or cheerleading. The smallest comment may twist body image in a way never dreamed or intended.
- If students need to be removed from a team or class until they meet weight requirements, don't desert them. Keep in touch and encourage their teammates and classmates to maintain their friendships.

STEROIDS

Every teenager dreams of playing in the NFL like Peyton Manning, riding a bike in the Tour de France like Lance Armstrong, or triumphing in the Olympics like Jackie Joyner-Kersee. For 4% to 6% of high school senior boys and 1% to 3% of high school senior girls, making this dream come true involves the use of performance-enhancing steroids. Athletes are given a distinct advantage with this synthetic form of the male hormone testosterone. The fact that steroids are illegal and unfair in competition is often lost in the roaring cheer of the crowd.

Steroids do not just enhance the muscle mass of the athlete, which teenagers view as a positive; there is also a distinct negative side to using this synthetic substance. Steroid use is associated with sterility, stunted growth, and severe mood swings. It steers the hypothalamus and limbic areas of the brain into overdrive. It ignites aggression, hostility, and anger, along with other negative and counterproductive emotions. Teenage athletes on steroids are primed to argue with teammates, coaches, and anyone else who gets in their way.

There is concern that steroids may permanently change the brain's wiring, making impulse control a lifelong issue. Teens who engage in this chemical abuse tend to use heavier steroids as they get older, which sets the stage for other illegal drug use. Additionally, steroid use has been linked to health problems such as heart attacks, stroke, and liver cancer.

The bulking of a teen's body should make steroid use fairly evident, but it you are unsure, speak to a professional about what signs to look for. Speak with your school's athletic director, coaches, and administrators. An adult needs to openly ask a teenager if he or she is taking steroids. Strongly recommend counseling and consider regular drug testing.

SLEEP

Remember the six-year-old who couldn't wait to wake up at 7:00 a.m., eat a bowl of cereal, and watch cartoons? Now she's the 16-year-old who wants to sleep until noon and has to be dragged out of bed each morning. What happened? First of all, adolescents need approximately one more hour of sleep each night than adults do. Second, melatonin, nature's sleeping pill, is released at a different time in the brain of

teenagers. This results in teens sleeping later in the morning and drift-
ing off to sleep later at night.

The amount of sleep that one gets affects the way that one thinks,
acts, and looks. With the best of intentions, parents may insist that a
teenager hit the sack at what they consider an appropriate time, but they
should not be surprised to learn that their teen spends the time wide
awake, staring at the ceiling. Adolescents cannot fall asleep just because their parents said so.

Parents can cater to teen sleeping patterns on the weekends, but the
real world does not revolve around the teen's natural sleeping schedule.
Unfortunately, about 20% of teens are severely sleep deprived. The
consequences of sleep deprivation are severe. Teens who are experiencing exhaustion have more difficulty focusing and learning at school
and are prone to having overemotional reactions to stressors. The sleep-
deprived teen will burst into tears or become argumentative with little
provocation, suddenly crying over a forgotten book or slugging someone for sitting in a saved seat. Sleep deprivation also leads to the body's
experiencing difficulty in processing glucose, which results in excessive weight gain and obesity.

Teachers have little to no control over the sleep habits of their students. A teacher's only line of defense is to make students and their parents aware of research on sleep and to offer suggestions.

Tips for parents:

- Parents and teens should know that calming activities right before
  bed set the stage for snoozing. Get teens into the habit of reading
  a book, listening to music, or journaling. These types of activities
  help them relax mentally and physically. Nighttime is not the time
  to exercise, watch a thriller, or get into an argument.
- Arguing about bedtime at bedtime (a too-common occurrence)
  simply exacerbates the problem.
- If teens are sleep deprived, make gradual changes in their sleep
  patterns, perhaps changing their bedtimes as gradually as 10 minutes a week. Small increments have been shown to be effective in
  changing sleep schedules.
- To aid in sound sleeping, keep the room as dark as possible, with
  heavy shades and no nightlight (unless they really do need one).

- Binge sleeping on the weekends does not solve long-term sleep problems; however, suggest that parents allow teens to sleep in. They will love them for it.

If teens fall asleep in class, begin by talking to them to find out why. Is it a job, family, or too much fun? Many students are trying to work — sometimes to help support their families (an unfortunate but honorable cause), sometimes to help support their car payments (an unfortunate priority). Explore with them alternatives inside or outside of class that may allow them to get those much-needed *zzzz*s. They need an adult's problem-solving brain to entertain options and help them make good choices. Preliminary research on standardized tests suggests that mid-morning and early afternoon are the optimum time frames to assess teenagers, increasing scores on high-stakes tests.

Informed and proactive schools are setting later start times for middle school and high school students. If you're politically inclined, start a discussion about this with your local school board. The research will support you. Not only would teens do better in school with a later start, but the majority of juvenile crime and teenage pregnancy incidents occur between 3:00 and 6:00 p.m. (when parents are working and kids are unsupervised). School hours that extend later into the afternoon would shield them from risky temptations.

CHAPTER 8

Meeting Special Challenges

Individual experiences, personal temperament, and chemicals gone awry—they all affect adolescent learning. Research on the brain is pointing to sources and solutions that reach and teach students who are facing troubling challenges.

Did you know that . . .

- Attention Deficit Hyperactivity Disorder (ADHD) adolescents have difficulty understanding cause and effect?
- words can wound the brain?
- infants pattern their brains after their main caretakers' brains?
- cutting relieves tension?
- students in poverty feel more stress and have fewer calming agents in their brains?

ATTENTION DEFICIT HYPERACTIVITY DISORDER

"My sister had four 'underages' before she was 16—I blame it on her ADHD. School wasn't accommodating—she couldn't sit there. She was always in trouble; her grades suffered. The teachers were always saying, 'She has lots more potential' and crap like that. She felt outside of everything, felt like she didn't have any friends that understood her. In school, when she was supposed to take meds over lunch, she wouldn't go because she didn't want to look different. She felt displaced. So, she started into the alcohol and drug scene—she'd even do it in front of me. She'd smoke pot in her room. I was in the middle of it; I'd watch her get high, and she'd say things like, 'I'm going to sneak out—don't tell mom and dad.'

"She didn't know that my dad always had ADHD; they would butt heads all the time. My parents tried everything. They put her in treatment, lots of counseling. Junior year of high school, she started going to an alternative school, and she thrived there. She could switch activities whenever she wanted, and they only went to one in the afternoon. She graduated with honors—amazing for her." These are words from a girl describing the life of her older sister who had ADHD during high school.

Imagine every aggravating, normal teenage tendency: impulsivity, risk taking, argumentativeness. Now, multiply that by 100, and you have a teenager with ADHD. Uncontrolled ADHD is life limiting. Teenagers with ADHD have high dropout rates, enter into turbulent friendships, and change jobs impulsively.

Because of a short attention span, students with ADHD struggle with the concept of time and sequencing. This becomes a real problem during the teen years, when the expectation is that one is old enough to manage one's own time. If the ADHD teen is told to be at basketball practice at 4:00 p.m., it is not uncommon for him or her to show up an hour late. The reason is tied much more to ADHD than disobedience. ADHD adolescents are busy playing computer games, skateboarding, and listening to music, and the last thing they are paying attention to is the time. To top it off, they have difficulty understanding sequencing and its cause-and-effect nature. They get detention for turning in homework late, but they continue to not turn in work in a timely manner, not making the connection between detention and late homework.

Grappling with sequencing makes it difficult for them to get away with anything. An ADHD teen may drink part of a parent's bottle of wine and be surprised when confronted about it. How did Mom and Dad know? It never dawns on the teenager that because half the wine is gone and because Mom and Dad know that they didn't drink it, there are few likely culprits other than the teen. Being sneaky is not an ADHD teen's strength.

"I don't know" is a constant mantra of ADHD teenagers. Part of this stems from problems with sequencing, and part of it comes from not being able to focus on anything for an extended period. You ask them to do a written assignment: They start to do it, get distracted by a mechanical pencil on their desk, decide to talk to the girl next to them, practice tapping on their desk that song that they just can't get out of their head, and look for that planner they've been missing. When asked 30 minutes later why they haven't done their work, they can sincerely say that they don't know. And the truth is, they don't. The answer is down a straight path, but their mind has wandered down a crooked lane.

It's also common for them to hyperfocus, an act where attention is intensely directed to one activity. At school, they may be so intent on surfing the Internet that they fail to notice that the teacher has told them five times that it's time to log off. Hyperfocusing is particularly prevalent in activities that move at a quick pace and require immediate responses, activities such as playing computer games and instant messaging are ripe for this response. Interrupting ADHD teens that are hyperfocusing will always result in an explosive clash. This reaction should come as no surprise; all energy is being expended on one task, and any disruption is beyond their level of frustration. They are not hesitant to show their rage to teachers, parents, and peers. They are quick to lose control and slow in gaining it back. Once ADHD teenagers have lost emotional control, they usually become more argumentative and aggressive than other teens.

There is clear evidence that there is a biological difference between the brains of ADHD individuals and those of others. This neuroscientific proof should help take the blame off teachers, parents, and ADHD teenagers for their inappropriate behavior. For many years, it was thought that if teachers and parents would just lay down the law or if the teenager would just pay attention, all the nonsense would stop. Now, we know better.

There are many abnormalities in the brain of individuals with ADHD. Brain size is about 3% to 4% smaller in teenagers with ADHD as compared to their age mates without it. The smaller the brain, the more severe the ADHD (but size does not affect intelligence). The basal ganglia, a part of the brain associated with thinking and emotion, has reduced activity, as do areas in the frontal lobes. Not surprisingly, the areas in the frontal lobes that control attention and impulse are smaller and less active in teenagers with ADHD.

When working with ADHD students, stay calm and then stay calm again. Expect overreactions. When they explode, remove them from the room, and turn a deaf ear to their tirade. It's not uncommon to have to become deaf for a 1- or 2-minute outburst. Do not get off topic. Do not defend yourself. These responses won't help the teenager get under control, and they usually result in his or her behavior escalating. Your best bet is to wait and then simply restate your original request in a quiet and nonconfrontational tone.

It is well established that there is an overreliance on hyperactive drugs to control students. However, if a proper diagnosis is made by a physician who specializes in ADHD, medication can make the difference between intolerable behavior and acceptable conduct. Teachers are in a unique position to track behaviors that give parents and physicians a clear school picture upon which to base decisions.

Instructional strategies:

- Maintaining attention in the academic setting requires deliberate effort with ADHD students. Try to reduce distractions—seat them near the front of the room, clear their desks of objects, and keep their desks away from high-traffic areas.
- Transitions between activities are particularly difficult for ADHD students. Assist them by positioning yourself in close proximity to them, and give directions one step at a time.
- Break assignments into smaller portions to reduce their feelings of being overwhelmed.
- Help ADHD students recognize their academic progress with short-term, specific goals.
- Computers (with their capability for quick input and responses) draw the ADHD students' attention. This is an effective way to offer instruction.
- Help their disorganized minds become organized by teaching them study skills and how to use planners.

ABUSED TEENS

Sadly, everyone can point to flagrant examples of child neglect and abuse. The one that is burned into my mind is Lance. He was 14 when

I met him. He had moved across country to live with his mother and older brother after years of sexual abuse from his father. Ninety percent of the time Lance was pleasant and hard working, but the remaining time, he was explosive and unmanageable. His volatility meant continual problems in school with teachers and peers.

A conversation with his mother illuminates how unstable his home life was. For his birthday, Lance's father sent him a box of pornography. His mother intercepted it but after some convoluted consideration, decided to give it to him, explaining to me that "it was a gift from his father."

The school and community tried to help Lance but to no avail. He became involved in the world of prostitution as a pimp, which eventually led him to the correctional system. The last time I spoke with him, it was clear that he had no grounding as to what was right or wrong behavior.

Ongoing research suggests that the adolescent brain is far more dynamic and susceptible to the effects of good and bad experiences than was previously thought. EEG and fMRI imaging have provided neuroscientists with evidence that physical and sexual abuse that occurs during adolescence leaves scars apparent in the adult brain. The left hemisphere of the brain, the limbic system, and the corpus callosum are particularly affected and show abnormal activity in abused people. In the real world, these individuals demonstrate more difficulty handling stress.

Researchers are now beginning to view the impact of verbal abuse on teenagers, too. They speculate that the stress caused by repeatedly being exposed to cruel words wounds the brain.

If a student comes to you and claims that he or she was abused, take that student seriously. Besides the fact that you are legally bound to report this to authorities, the teen may risk exposing his or her predator only once. You are in the position of learning valuable, helpful information. If you suspect that abuse is happening but a teen says nothing, speak to the school counselor and administrator. Someone should be designated to ask that teen directly. Realize that an abuse victim may not answer truthfully at first, whether out of shame or embarrassment. Physical and sexual abuse is a life-altering and life-threatening experience that requires the aid of professionals; recommend help from a trained therapist for diagnosis and treatment.

REACTIVE ATTACHMENT DISORDER

Bonding is a requirement for a healthy baby brain, and this process takes time. Babies take 2 years to bond with their parents and guardians. Bonding is the connection between the primary caregiver and the baby as the former meets the latter's needs. Being fed when hungry, receiving a breast or a bottle when thirsty, having wet diapers changed, being given blankets for warmth, and being rocked and held when upset are the way that babies bond with their mothers. A lack of bonding may be caused by premature birth, abuse (physical, emotional, or sexual), neglect, frequent separation from caretaker (foster children are particularly vulnerable), and maternal depression—all situations that result in infants not being nurtured in the first few months and years of life.

Babies build their brains around their mothers. They pattern their brains and learn to fire their brains as their mothers do. Without the template of their moms' brains, babies are dependent on the emotional amygdala. It is hypothesized that the prefrontal cortex of the mom becomes the prefrontal cortex of the baby—it's rational and logical thinking helps organize emotions.

The lack of bonding takes a mighty toll on the brain. Dramatic but pertinent examples are the Romanian orphans who were neglected in orphanages and then adopted by parents in the United States. Groups of these babies were studied and found to have 20% smaller brains than those of their infant counterparts in the United States. Equally disconcerting was that fMRI scans of their brains showed large areas with no activity. Put into enriched homes at young ages where they were fed, changed, and cuddled, these children were able to attain average intelligence. This shows the impact of a positive environment, and it has direct implications for teachers.

Criminals, young or old, have a high incidence of reactive attachment disorder (RAD). PET scans show that men in prison have smaller right hemispheres than do men who are not incarcerated—this is another indicator of RAD. The right hemisphere is the part of the brain responsible for the regulation of affect. It develops quickly during the first 18 months of life, and it is dependent on a connection with the main caregiver.

Many juvenile delinquents are identified as having RAD. They are in a constant struggle to try to control their shaky, unstable worlds in hopes of ensuring their own survival. Adults are not seen as being safe or friendly, but why should they be? No adult met their needs when they were helpless babies.

Characteristics of individuals with RAD:

- Manipulative
- Often engage in power struggles—they want to push teachers' buttons and make them mad
- Lie to your face (often, the only time they establish eye contact is when they lie)—they will say they turned in homework even when it is clearly still sitting on their desks
- Preoccupation with fire, blood, and gore—they self-inflict wounds and hurt pets
- Difficulty keeping friends

In the classroom, be consistent and specific with directions; leave no room for misunderstandings. If they try to flip your switch by lying or accusing you or their peers of misconduct, remain calm and in control. If you lose control, they will be in control of the situation, and they are not up to the task. Do not allow such students to be alone with you; they are manipulative and will not hesitate to accuse you of inappropriate behavior.

Document your concerns and communicate them to their parents. Parental reactions tend to go the full range from relief that someone is finally seeing the same type of behaviors that they have been living with, to defensive responses that they aren't to blame. No matter what their initial reaction, try to work with parents to best meet the needs of these students.

Unfortunately, the prognosis is not good for teenagers with RAD; they are at high risk for dropping out of school and for ending up in correctional facilities (see chapter 10). The immediate feedback found in behavior management programs is often an effective tool when working with students with RAD. They benefit from immediate consequences for poor behavior and from rewards for positive behavior. A clear and direct line between their actions and consequences is a part of rewiring their brains.

CUTTING

Abby was 13 when she began cutting. She came from what seemed like a normal albeit controlling family, but little did anyone know what torments haunted Abby at home. Although both parents were overly controlling, her mother crossed the line into being cruel and destructive. What seemed like kooky, busy-bee behavior to her friends turned into erratic and irrational behavior toward her children. She would fly off the handle with little provocation.

The constant criticism and unhappiness at home led Abby to begin cutting herself. The first time she cut herself, she described it as "a relief" that she "finally had a way to calm down." Every week, she made small cuts on her arms and stomach. Concerned about hiding her cuts, she said, "I was always worried about summer: swimsuits, summer tops. Someone could find out." Interestingly, many of Abby's friends knew about her cutting, but no one ever said anything to an adult. It wasn't until she was 18 that she began to open up about her unhealthy coping skill.

Cutting, a form of self-injury, is nothing new, but like so many dirty little secrets, it's only now coming to the light of day. It is an exterior expression of an interior pain. The majority of cutters are young girls between the ages of 13 and 15. They usually use a razor to cut the skin and cause bleeding, but they do not directly hit a vein or artery to trigger life-threatening injury.

It is theorized that boys explode and girls implode. Young teenage girls use cutting as a means of handling strong emotion and relieving tension and stress. Cutting becomes a way of speaking when no words will come. In the case of abuse, the pain of cutting takes away the numbness that teen girls feel in their lives. In some cases, it is used as self-punishment for feelings of guilt. Cutting is most commonly found where there has been sexual abuse, physical and emotional neglect, and family dysfunction.

The reason for cutting is environmental, but there is also a brain connection. Researchers have found that serotonin, a calming agent, is not properly used in a cutter's brain. Theory has it that the cuts release endorphins, the body's natural painkillers, thereby creating feelings of pleasure.

Be savvy. Most cutters feel shame and go to great lengths to hide their cuts. Take note if teenagers always wear long sleeves, even when it doesn't make sense, such as during hot weather or while bathing. The copycat nature of teenage behavior makes it a special concern in middle school. Once a girl begins to cut, her friends become intrigued and experiment with it themselves.

If a teen confesses to you about her cutting, validate her feelings. You don't have to approve of the behavior, but you do need to acknowledge that it's okay to feel upset, overwhelmed, or depressed. Cutters do not have healthy coping skills. They are not dealing with intense emotions in an appropriate way. Be a good role model, and exhibit or suggest healthy ways of coping with stress and other high emotions.

Talk to the parents of cutters and recommend a counselor or therapist. Professional intervention is necessary; cutting is associated with depression and anorexia and puts such teens at high risk. There is preliminary research that medications that reduce depression and anxiety may also help cutters; a therapist will be able to advise parents and teenagers about this possible treatment.

There are many websites designed as support groups for teens that cut. Don't be surprised if teenagers find meaningful connections online. This is their world, and so it should come as no shock that they look to technology for emotional support. The sites are available 24 hours a day, a bonus for the emotional insomniac. Parents should check out the website to make sure that it is appropriate and that it addresses solutions rather than compound the problem.

RUNAWAYS

Tasha, a basically good girl, was in eighth grade when she and a few friends decided to run away from home. (No one can pinpoint what prompted this decision.) They started by grabbing all the chips, salsa, and junk food they could find around Tasha's house; then, they hit the road. They were sure that the good times were about to roll. The plan was to drive from Sioux Falls, South Dakota, to Minneapolis–Saint Paul (a 5-hour drive). They had no plan for what they would do once they arrived in the Twin Cities; they were taking things as they came, throwing caution to the wind. Four hours later, they found themselves in Luverne, a 30-minute drive from Sioux Falls. Relying only on their senses of direction, they had been driving in circles.

Exhausted from driving, they began brainstorming what to do next. They decided to crash at a house belonging to some young adults whom they knew in Sioux Falls. They spent the next week "watching television, drinking alcohol, and just hangin' around," never reflecting on the pain and worry they were causing their parents. As fate would have it, the house they chose to stay in was across the street from their middle school. Peers saw them playing outside and reported them to the school authorities. The information was quickly followed up on, and the girls were reunited with their families. This time, there was a happy ending, which isn't always the case with runaways.

The legal system spreads a wide net in its definition of runaways; any minor that leaves home for one night without parent or guardian permission falls under the definition. Until 1974 it was considered a crime, but understanding and compassion now reigns, and runaways are viewed in a kinder and more empathetic light.

Runaways usually show signs of stress before leaving home—delinquency, depression, and academic and behavioral difficulties in school. Running away is often associated with family problems such as an alcoholic parent, incest, and violence, but there are other factors that play into teenagers' leaving home. Arguments over curfew, disapproval of a boyfriend or girlfriend, low grades, disagreements over dress and hairstyle, pregnancy, and homosexuality have all been documented as reasons for teens' leaving home. Individual factors may also play a role. An emotionally disturbed teenager may turn to the streets, as might a teenager who idealizes the world or is searching for excitement. The reasons for teenage runaways run the full span, from serious and horrific to minor and exasperating.

Poor decision making, impulsivity, the inability to envision the future, and a lack of problem-solving abilities all lead to the choice of running away. The immature frontal lobes and the overactive amygdala put the adolescent at high risk for deciding that of all their options, running away is the best one.

The number of teenagers who run away is increasing in the United States. Once on the street, their lives are in a precarious position with potentially serious consequences. Basic needs such as food, shelter, and medical care are not easily available. Over half of runaways turn to prostitution within one month of leaving home; 65% are sexually active, and a high percentage contract AIDS or STDs. Depression is common, as is low self-esteem, which puts them at high risk for suicide.

Schools can provide support by offering programs that explain the problems and causes of running away. Viable options to running away need to be put front and center in the discussion. Seeking help from a trusted teacher, school counselor, family therapist, or religious leader is in teens' best interest.

POVERTY

Poverty, those deprived of financial resources and power, translates into limited experiences for children and teenagers. A lack of enrichment and experiences means reduced dendrites and synaptic connections in the brain. Children born into poverty miss an opportunity to increase their brainpower right from birth. They have fewer experiences than do preschoolers from middle-class homes. They enter kindergarten with underdeveloped vocabularies, and this deficiency haunts them into their teenage years.

Medical care, safety, dysfunctional families, substance abuse, and violence are all bitter companions of poverty, causing negative emotions of fear and stress to permeate the teenager's brain. When under stress, the brain goes into survival mode, and reading, writing, and arithmetic are lost in the chaos. Paying attention, learning the content, and taking a test take a backseat to ensuring safety and basic necessities.

Unfortunately, fear of failure, isolation, and trauma—often present in teens living in poverty—causes dopamine to be converted into norepinephrine. Norepinephrine energizes an individual and, under adverse conditions, results in aggression and agitation. Researchers have found that individuals in poverty have less serotonin in their bodies, which contributes to feelings of unrest and anxiety. This makes it difficult for them to tolerate any additional frustration and stress in their lives. Impoverished students may become argumentative or they may just give up when things get tough in school.

Poverty is a societal problem, but teachers have individual power. Factors that protect and improve resiliency for students living in poverty include the following:

- A stable, positive emotional relationship with at least one responsible adult
- Average or above-average intelligence
- Past success to build a foundation for future success
- Active coping skills—impoverished teens seek to solve their own problems or overcome challenges
- A positive temperament (a largely inborn trait)—these teens are active and social, not passive and isolated
- An open and supportive educational and social climate at school and home
- Neighborhood and community support
- A sense of humor
- Caring for others
- Problem-solving skills
- The ability to find alternate solutions
- Critical reasoning skills
- High self-esteem
- Impulse control
- Planning ability
- Goal-setting capability

CHAPTER 9

Addiction: Alcohol, Drugs, and Smoking

The imperfect escape—smoking, alcohol, meth, cocaine all provide a foggy and hazy drugged-filled reality for teenagers. The teen is eager to taste-test and sample each and every one of these potentially hazardous compulsions, often with disastrous consequences. Did you know that . . .

- the adolescent brain becomes addicted faster than the adult brain?
- the adolescent brain is more resistant to treatment than the adult brain?
- excessive drinking causes the brain to lose short-term memory?
- mothers who smoke while pregnant put their future adolescents at high risk for becoming addicted to cigarettes?

It had snowed all weekend, and Will and his friends were chomping at the bit to get outside and have some fun. The plan was to meet at a local field to sled. Will decided to add to the fun by bringing along vodka and cherry Coke; before long, all the boys had drunk too much, and suddenly, it seemed like a good idea to tie an inner tube to a car with 20 feet of rope. One bad decision led to another, and before long, the boys stripped down to their skivvies. They then took turns pulling each other in a car around the snowy field in their boxers. Knees, arms, and chests were scraped, but fortunately, no serious injury resulted.

Experimenting with alcohol is not unusual for teenagers. For some, it's testing the waters, a bit of tiptoeing on the dark side. For others, it becomes a serious problem. It's important for teachers and parents to not overreact and to take each case on an individual basis. John, for example, was sent to a treatment center after a single drinking episode; this was not in his best interest, and it compounded his problems.

THE BRAIN'S ROLE IN ADDICTION

The fierce grip of addiction can seize a person at any age, but the adolescent is particularly vulnerable. A variety of factors determine an individual's susceptibility to addiction, such as environment (stress from school, peers, and parents), personal genetics (alcoholism runs in the family), and the brain. During adolescence, the brain is sensitive to addiction. That is, exposure to an addictive substance has a more powerful and detrimental effect during adolescence than at other times. As a result, teenagers who experiment with drugs or alcohol are more likely to become quickly addicted and to stay addicted. Neuroscientists believe that complex changes occurring in the brain during adolescence are responsible for this window of sensitivity.

Alcohol triggers a dopamine rush, causing those who consume it to relax and feel a natural high. As alcohol consumption becomes more frequent, the brain receives more dopamine and is tricked into believing that natural production of the neurotransmitter is unnecessary. As a result, natural dopamine production in the brain decreases. When people become addicted to alcohol, their brain no longer produces adequate levels of dopamine, and they are unable to experience natural highs. The exuberance that one feels when seeing a touchdown, the joy of seeing a longtime friend are diminished in the addict's brain. To feel good, the addict must rely on alcohol. Other addictive substances produce the same result.

Substance abuse and addiction are particularly harmful to the frontal lobes and hippocampus. Excessive drinking causes the hippocampus to shrink, thereby limiting short-term memory. Addicted teens have trouble remembering what they did the night before, who they were with, and where they went. Researchers believe that one binge-drinking episode can impair a teen's memory for up to 30 days. This means that although the hippocampus is recovering, a teen will not learn as much in school as he or she would otherwise. Fortunately, short-term memory is resilient and eventually restores itself when given a chance to recover.

The frontal lobes, the parts of the brain responsible for good decision making, are also profoundly affected by drinking. The frontal lobes are not fully developed during adolescence, thus rendering a teen's ability to make good decisions a tenuous one at best. This problem is compounded when a teen consumes alcohol, which lowers inhibitions. Although it is common for people of any age to become less inhibited when they drink (you've seen them at karaoke night), teens are more likely to completely throw caution to the wind and engage in reckless and risky behavior, such as unsafe sexual activity, drag racing, and fighting—all of which can have disastrous results.

And teenagers are more likely to drink to excess than adults are. The reason is that the body's physical signs that it has ingested too much alcohol do not manifest themselves as quickly in a teenager as they do in an adult. Although adults will quickly begin to slur their words, stumble, and become sleepy, teens don't receive these signals until much later. As a result, teens will consume dangerous levels of alcohol before their bodies send the signal that they are intoxicated.

Not only is the brain more susceptible to addiction during the teenage years, but it is also much more resistant to treatment. The statistics on recovery make it clear that overcoming any addiction is an arduous task, but for those who become addicted in their teen years, the battle is uphill and lifelong.

Finally, addiction may be a particularly troubling problem for girls. Recent research shows that adolescent girls are more susceptible to the effects of alcohol than their male counterparts are. These studies show that teen girls who frequently drink are at an increased risk for behavioral problems and have more neural abnormalities than boys do.

Michelle is one girl who suffered the serious consequences of teenage addiction. She began running with the wrong crowd at the end of middle school. She started dating older boys, and before she knew it, her boyfriend introduced her to methamphetamine. Meth is a relentless drug that soon took over her mind, body, and soul. She moved out of her home, attended school sporadically, and was out of touch with

family for months at a time. Her parents eventually resigned themselves to the fact that the addiction would kill her.

Teachers gave her chance after chance to perform in school, but the addiction always won. She dropped out, attended an alternative school for
a while, and, amazingly and to her credit, was able to earn her GED. At
age 19, she was picked up for possession and attempting to sell drugs,
and she spent 6 months in prison—ironically, the longest period that she
had been clean in years. Hoping that she had learned her lesson and with
the best of intentions, her parents enrolled her in college. The freedom
and stresses involved in college life quickly drove her back to the streets.
In hindsight, a halfway house for addicts that provided supervision and
strict enforcement of rules and regulations would have been a better
choice for Michelle. Sadly, her family has not seen her in months.

SMOKING

Although it seems like a less dangerous addiction, smoking is another
problem that starts in adolescence. The majority of smokers begin the
habit before they are 21 years old. Similar to other addictive substances, nicotine furnishes a seductive dopamine rush. Smoking is
quickly hardwired into the teenage brain and, as most would attest,
quite resistant to change.

Disturbing research warns that teens whose mothers smoke during
pregnancy can show signs of nicotine dependence after just five cigarettes. Sadly, the damage done to the brain during the prenatal period
makes these teenagers vulnerable to nicotine addiction years later. And
just as with drugs and alcohol, teen brains are hardwired to the addiction, making quitting a grueling affair. Other factors play in the choice
to puff or not puff; parental modeling, peers, and teenage experimentation are indisputable influences.

THE ROLE OF EDUCATORS

Teenagers that come to school under the influence should be immediately removed from the classroom. Discussion with a teenager who is
high on drugs or alcohol is unproductive and futile—save your breath.

Instead, send him or her directly to the office, and let school policy go into motion. Ideally, school policy includes more than punishment. Teens with addictions require support groups such as Al-Anon or Alateen to put recovery into motion. The addiction needs to be tended to before the focus sets on academics.

If there is an alcohol- or drug-related tragedy at school or in the community, listen to students' thoughts and encourage them to talk. This is no time for a lecture. Allow teens to draw their own conclusions. Meeting with counselors and establishing safe places for students to meet and talk with one another immediately after the painful event provides important support.

Signs that indicate a possible chemical dependency issue:

- Dishonesty with peers about drinking or using
- Friends that are known to have addiction problems
- Low self-esteem
- Hangovers
- Frequent mood changes
- Drop in school grades
- Memory loss
- Loss of friends
- Withdrawal from normal activities
- Acting defensive when confronted
- Getting fired from jobs
- Frequent broken promises

The teenager with an addiction problem needs treatment, and the sooner the better. Consider the following before selecting a treatment facility:

- Separation of juveniles and adults
- Available group and individual counseling, with frequent treatment schedules
- A significant percentage of recovery and certified staff
- Whether the program offers continued professional support once a patient leaves the facility

CHAPTER 10

One More Chance: Education in Juvenile Correctional Facilities

Juvenile correctional facilities are often the last hope for academic achievement. For many juveniles, these facilities mean regular meals, clean clothes, a safe harbor, and school for the first time in a long time. These students' brains have been wired in a destructive manner, and rewiring can be a lifelong challenge.

Did you know that . . .

- the majority of incarcerated youth read between the third- and seventh-grade level?
- 42% of juveniles in correctional facilities are emotionally and behaviorally disturbed and that many have additional mental and emotional issues?
- juvenile delinquents benefit from service to the community?
- juvenile delinquents need to rewire their brains?

JUVENILE DELINQUENCY

Upon entering a new correctional facility, it is customary for delinquents to write their biographies, explaining and reflecting on what brought them to the facility in the first place. Gary had been in trouble with the law since he was 11 years old, and he wrote a long essay describing the bright spots and stumbling blocks of his life. He wrote in detail about his parents, who had both been in prison for as long as he could remember. He had grown up with his maternal grandmother. He fondly recalled a happy childhood, playing with friends, going to school, and riding his bike. He had a general feeling that his life was on track until, as he put it, "Grandma knifed somebody; she got sent to prison."

Gary soon found himself in the correctional system, and by age 16, he had spent the last 5 years in and out of facilities. He is considered *institutionalized*—he knows no other life. Gary's story is one that mirrors many of the boys' and girls' lives in corrections.

The statistics surrounding juvenile correctional facilities are grim at best: Recidivism rates are high; truancy is high; and the majority have repeated a grade in school. As mentioned, the average reading level for adolescent offenders is between third and seventh grade, and the average math scores are at the sixth-grade level.

Many of these students have emotional and social challenges. According to the latest Office of Special Education Programs' annual survey from the U.S. Department of Education, fewer than 1% of the students in K–12 public schools are identified as having emotional disorders. The percentage is alarmingly higher in correctional facilities, with 42% of the population being classified as emotionally and behaviorally disturbed (see the chapter 5 section Emotionally and Behaviorally Disturbed Students) and large numbers being identified with ADHD (see the chapter 8 section Attention Deficit Hyperactivity Disorder), conduct disorder, and oppositional defiance disorder.

To say that educators' work is cut out for them is an understatement. Ensuring academic proficiency with juvenile delinquents is a special challenge to teachers and administrators.

LEGAL CULPABILITY

Contrary to the mantra of "I didn't do it," teenagers do commit crimes—impulsive crimes. They are not drawn to crimes that require a great deal of premeditation or brutality. Juveniles are drawn to crimes such as theft, arson, vandalism, simple assault, and disorderly conduct. These crimes contain an element of the rash decision making and knee-jerk reactions that are prevalent in the teenage brain.

The world of drugs holds a special spot in the juvenile delinquent's heart. Selling and snorting provide the ability to make fast money while getting high, a euphoric combination. This is largely due to a combination of teens' inability to comprehend long-term consequences, their irresistible attraction to novelty, and their limited coping skills.

On the upside, teenagers commit a relatively small number of violent crimes. This may come as a surprise to many because the media often paints a different, more sensationalized picture than the actual truth does. Painfully, 80% of teens who commit murder kill the person who is abusing their mother; this is important information for social workers, guardian ad litems, and others that are in a position of being proactive.

The United States, along with most countries worldwide, decreed capital punishment for crimes committed by juveniles to be illegal. This decision was partially based on the condition of the teenage frontal lobe. Credible evidence proved that teenagers have an inability to foresee consequences and to control impulses. They do not possess an adult brain and therefore should not be given adult consequences. Fortunately, many juvenile offenders grow out of their criminal behavior and stop committing crimes as they become adults.

CURRICULUM

One new teacher at a correctional facility related the story of teaching delinquents current events that dealt with a crime that involved an athlete at the local college. As they read the article, difficult vocabulary words were discussed for meaning. The first word that the teacher asked them to describe was *fundamental*; no one knew what it meant. The next difficult word was *acute*, and once again, no one knew the meaning. The third difficult phrase was *change of venue*. The teacher asked the meaning of the words, and much to his surprise, every hand in the room went up—living proof that vocabulary has everything to do with past experience.

Just as with at-risk students in the regular schools, creating a sense of belonging and bonding is the first order of business in a correctional facility. The brain responds at an emotional level to safety and acceptance. Because of their histories, students in corrections need more time to bond with stable adults. Surprisingly, the constant revolving-door nature of correctional facilities adds to the at-risk factors. Transferring juveniles from facility to facility or going between home and facility is not necessarily ideal; it is important for them to stay in one place long enough to bond with significant adults.

The curriculum in correctional facilities mirrors that of the regular school. The education program centers on the core curriculum of language arts, math, science, and social studies. In addition, drug and alcohol prevention, social skills (see chapter 4), life skills, and anger management are a significant part of these programs. A major goal of teachers, line staff, and program managers in these facilities is to get the teenager to think differently. Their brains are wired in a destructive manner, and they need direct instruction to think differently.

Suggested curriculum and strategies:

- Provide direct instruction in reading and math.
- Embed multiple-intelligence strategies into instruction. Reading and writing skills are often not juveniles' strength; MI allows these students to build on other areas and reduce frustration.
- Schedule physical education daily—it reduces stress, and it benefits the emotional part of the brain.
- Implement individual, small group, and large group instruction to meet the needs of the students. It is not uncommon to find reading abilities ranging from third grade to 12th grade in one class. To meet the range of needs in a class, individualized instruction is desired. At the same time, students greatly benefit from learning to work with others in a group and to properly attend to large group instruction.
- Life skills focused on transition into the workforce is a valued and important component in the education program. In many cases, because of off-campus restrictions, shadowing and internships may be subject to limitations. This does not preclude a vigorous emphasis in the curriculum on how to get and hold a job.
- Projects with hand-on activities are academically sound and motivating. These students have had few experiences with abstract thought, and they benefit from accompanying the abstract with the concrete. Realize, however, that these projects can take on lives of their own in a correctional facility.

One teacher who was doing a unit on the solar system decided to have the boys make paper-mache planets to have a 3-D visual of the content. The unit was designed to last one week. One month later, they were putting the finishing touches on their planets. A mixture of boys coming and going, court appointments, speakers at the facility, farmers wanting them to work in the fields, overexcitement, and lack of focus resulted in the lesson plans taking much longer than anticipated. Still, in the end, the results were glorious and the students were proud of their finished product.

- Periodically bring in exemplary adult convicts to talk about what they have learned from their life experiences. These adult mentors relate to the boys at a level that few others can, and they offer meaningful insights.
- Hold tests and quizzes to a minimum. These students have had so much school failure that it is important to reduce their anxiety levels for them to learn.
- Introduce needlepoint (the large plastic canvas) as a constructive stress reducer. When things start to go out of control, pull out the sewing. Designs of favorite sport teams' emblems are particular favorites.

OPPOSITIONAL DEFIANT DISORDER AND CONDUCT DISORDER

Leroy had had his share of run-ins with the law; when provoked, he was argumentative, drawn to violence, and identified as having conduct disorder. One cold winter morning in South Dakota, he decided to push the envelope. He waited on a corner for about an hour for a delivery man. When the man finally approached the convenience store, Leroy hit him with a pipe on the back of the head (fortunately, the hit was not too hard); the man fell to the ground, and Leroy snatched his money. He then began his carefully planned escape. He ran the four blocks to his car, stuck the key in the ignition, and turned it—*rhhhhhhhhhh*, nothing, *rhhhhhhh*, nothing. Leroy's car wouldn't start. He'd taken everything into consideration except the cold South Dakota weather. He was picked up before he could cover half a block running.

Leroy's actions were typical of a teen with conduct disorder. According to the *Diagnostic and Statistical Manual of Mental Disorders*, conduct disorder describes individuals who continually demonstrate behaviors that violate rules and the rights of others. The onset of conduct disorder is usually in late childhood or early adolescence, and it is much more prevalent in boys than it is in girls. These teenagers persistently act aggressively toward people and animals. They view pets as something to torture, not to care for and love.

As you might imagine, this causes significant problems in the teen's life with school, family, friends, and work. They may be reprimanded over and over for transgressions but don't seem to learn from the experience. Teenagers with conduct disorder misunderstand others and then react with aggression or threats, showing little or no remorse. They are easily frustrated and will regularly threaten suicide—a threat that should be taken seriously. Amazingly, about two thirds of people with conduct disorder stop this behavior in adulthood; the other one third have additional mental illnesses.

According to the manual, individuals with oppositional defiance disorder (ODD) also exhibit a negative pattern of hostile and defiant behavior. As with conduct disorder, it is more common in males than females. Adolescents with ODD show many of the same behaviors as those with conduct disorder do, but they don't tend to be mean or cruel. Instead, they are stubborn and disobedient. They are difficult to manage, but their behaviors are not as serious as are those of students with conduct disorder. Teens with ODD and conduct disorder often engage in other risk-taking activities, such as smoking, drugs, and alcohol.

The prefrontal cortex, involved in planning, decision making, and problem solving, does not work right in individuals with ODD and conduct disorder. When presented with memory tasks, the normal brain is active in the prefrontal cortex; individuals with conduct disorder and ODD do not show robust activity in this area of the brain. All other areas of the brain are similar for those with or without the disorder.

Possible causes of conduct disorder and ODD:

- One's temperament and the family's reaction to it
- Heredity—sometimes, it runs in families
- Neurological cause, such as a head injury

- Chemical imbalance in the brain (serotonin)
- Child abuse
- School failure
- Mother's smoking during pregnancy—nicotine disrupts fetal brain development

ANGER MANAGEMENT CLASSES

Rashad had been in the juvenile correctional facility for 2 days and was angry and belligerent. In class, he refused to do any work: He laid his head on his desk, would not respond to questions, and pushed papers away. The line staff asked him three times to sit up straight. The third time, Rashad exploded, starting with the words "You f— a—, you don't tell me what to do!" He then threw a book in the direction of the teacher and started for the door. At this point, two other line staff joined in a restraint, and he was removed from the classroom.

Another boy, Sean, purposely hit his nose with his fist and slammed his face into the wall to start a nosebleed. During a restraint, blood flew everywhere. When asked why he kept hurting himself, he said, "Nobody's gonna mess with me." Neither of these teenagers had logical responses or actions to anger.

Anger management is a common issue for most students in correctional facilities. In fact, it is so common that anger management classes are a routine and integral part of the curriculum. The underdeveloped prefrontal cortex and overly active amygdala are on a fighting spree, no holds barred. Tools provided in anger management classes encourage self-awareness, self-control, and empathy. These proactive strategies are effective combatants against substance abuse, bullying, and gang behavior.

Anger management classes are developed around the following principles:

- Recognizing anger and realizing that anger is a choice—answering questions such as, "What makes me angry? What people? What situations?" "Am I hurt? Afraid?" "When I'm angry, do I sweat? Clench my fists? Tighten my jaw?"

- Adapting realistic expectations for themselves and others—juveniles often believe that "others should have done this" or "that person didn't measure up." They need to replace those thoughts with "No one is perfect," " I need to give myself a break," or "He's a good friend."
- Controlling anger through breathing techniques ("Focus on breathing; take multiple deep breaths lasting 10 seconds"), talking and finding a safe space ("Find a safe person to vent to, and give yourself some time away from the anger-producing situation"), and exercise ("Jog, play basketball, exert physical energy to reduce stress").
- Communication skills—using *I* statements instead of *you* statements. This helps calm and redirect thinking, and it helps to deescalate the other person's negative emotions. Students learn to explain their thoughts, needs, and feelings in a way that doesn't anger and offend others.
- Developing problem-solving skills—in sequence, identify the problem, brainstorm alternative solutions, contemplate the consequences of each solution, select a solution, and reflect on the outcome.

CLASSROOM MANAGEMENT

A multifaceted classroom management style provides the best success in correctional facilities. A combination of a positive peer culture and behavior modification benefits students.

A positive peer culture focuses on self-responsibility, group responsibility, and authority responsibility. The goal is for students to be able to control and take responsibility for their behavior. If they are not able to exhibit this self-control, their peers step in and confront them and offer possible solutions. The targeted individuals then choose a solution from those offered by their peers. As a last resort, the authority figure steps in and guides the group. This is an intrinsically motivated program with embedded long-term life skills that ultimately take these students where they want to be.

An example of positive peer culture can be seen in a geography class. Bill, without physically touching another boy, was puffing out his

chest in a threatening manner and mouthing derogatory names. A class-
mate, Rico, warned Bill about his inappropriate manner. "Hey, stop
fronting," Rico said. Bill's behavior didn't stop, so one of the other
boys took the lead and said, "It's time for a RAP [response ability path-
ways]." The boys stopped their class work and formed a circle. They
were each given the opportunity to talk to Bill about his negative behavior in a calm and cooperative way. Bill took responsibility for his
actions, and the class returned to its normal studies. If Bill hadn't cho-
sen to take responsibility and rectify his actions, he would have been
removed from the classroom by the line staff.

Teacher behaviors that assist in maintaining classroom order:

- Stay calm and in control.
- Be helpful academically and emotionally.
- Have a sense of humor.
- Be fair.
- Give positive feedback.
- Don't engage in power struggles.

Behavior modification offers a structure with clear rules and immediate consequences to a mind that is ill-defined and wandering out of
control. It is an extrinsic program that stresses compliance, and it is
based on reinforcement for good behavior and punishment for bad behavior. Behavior modification helps students to learn how to

- Use self-time-outs.
- Identify trigger words.
- Identify actions that create anxiety and anger.
- Use coping skills.
- Get involved in physical activity as a healthy way to release en-
  ergy.
- Communicate.
- Utilize social skills (see chapter 4).
- Take responsibility.

One correctional facility had a half-baked behavior management
program implemented, which resulted in a great deal of chaos and bad

behaviors in the classroom. There is no doubt that staff and teachers were trying because boys were continually and consistently held accountable and punished for their behaviors. First, they walked laps, after which, they lost clothing privileges (i.e., they had to wear gray sweats), then shoe privileges (orange flip-flops), then no television and no games. There was no shortage of punishments; in fact, they seemed to be flying left and right.

The bad behaviors increased and increased. The reason became clear to the adults: The boys had nothing to lose after they lost all their privileges and rights. There was no incentive to be good. Identifying this as the problem did not mean that a solution was easy to ascertain.

To find one, the teachers, paraprofessionals, administrators, group leaders, and line staff met to brainstorm. After a number of meetings where they bounced around a variety of ideas, they decided that a behavior management program with positive behavior supports was the approach of choice. The premise behind such a program is that once a reward is earned, it cannot be taken away. As students progress through the program, they earn privileges. Students who exhibit bad behavior still have a consequence, but the consequence will not be the removal of earned rewards. Student behaviors immediately improved, and the boys continued to maintain good behavior over the long haul. The program was so successful that at the line staff's request, a modified version was implemented in the program's after-school hours.

The following is a sample of a behavior program used in the education program. In collaboration with each other, teachers and line staff track student behavior on an individual basis, class period by class period. Students start with a clear slate every morning and every afternoon, making the rewards more attainable.

Rewards for good behavior:

- Fifteen minutes of free time before lunch
- Thirty minutes of free time at end of the school day
- Food treats
- Five-minute free phone call
- Afternoon off school (although this one is a bit controversial)
- Movie
- Dinner off campus with line staff or teacher

Consequences for poor behavior:

- Warning
- Apology letter to teacher
- Loss of free time at lunch or at the end of the day
- Formal letter to juvenile correction agent or parole officer explaining behavior
- Thirty-minute detention

CONCLUSION

The behavior and academic achievement of juveniles often improve while they are in correctional facilities, but once released, they go back to the same friends, neighborhoods, and families that led them to their delinquent behavior. There are no national rates of recidivism for juveniles, but experts agree that it is a deep concern.

As a stand-alone entity, correctional facilities cannot make a significant dent in preventing future delinquent behavior. Halfway houses, group homes, and postadjudicated follow-up services are needed to ease the transition into society. These added supports make the difference between teens' connecting with old habits and their starting new lives in a positive direction.

Summary of Chapters

The more we know about the inner workings of the teenage brain, the more effective we will be as teachers and administrators. Thanks to a whole lot of neuroscientists expending a great deal of time and energy, there is more known about the teenage brain now than ever before. Their discoveries are complementing the work of psychologists and educationists to offer a more complete and accurate view of the adolescent.

CHAPTER 1—THE AT-RISK TEENAGE BRAIN

Teenagers are sprouting in more ways than one. Their brains are growing, fine-tuning, and marching to their owners' beat. We've always been aware of teens' wild and weird behavior, but it wasn't until recently that we realized the growth potential in the teenage brain.

In this chapter, you learned that . . .

- teenagers are learning information at an unprecedented rate;
- the good, the bad, and the ugly experiences that a teenager has determine what will grow in their brains;
- if information is not used by the brain, it is forgotten;
- a teen's engaging in one at-risk behavior increases the likelihood that he or she will become involved in other at-risk behaviors;
- some parts of the brain increase in efficiency by 100% during adolescence; and
- teen brains are more active than adult brains.

CHAPTER 2—TEACHING THE AT-RISK ADOLESCENT

In teaching at-risk students, the potential for success is high, but the obstacles are many. Meeting the needs of all students in a classroom is not easy, but if you add the challenges of the at-risk student, then a whole new chapter in teaching is launched.

In this chapter, you learned that . . .

- the teenage brain is particularly drawn to novelty to gain and keep attention, which increases the likelihood of risky behavior;
- the brain requires processing time to make sense of new information
- there is a big difference between a seventh grader's brain and a 12th grader's brain;
- the reasonable, logical, problem-solving areas of the brain are a work in progress;
- a multiple-intelligences approach to instruction stores information in various ways; and
- differentiating instruction aids in challenging students, not frustrating them.

CHAPTER 3—STAYING IN AND THRIVING IN SCHOOL

Dropping out of school is detrimental to students, families, and communities. There is nothing more rewarding than helping break the dropout cycle and providing a classroom environment where students can flourish academically, socially, and emotionally.

In this chapter, you learned that . . .

- teens have a difficult time organizing and remembering things;
- adolescents benefit from direct instruction on study strategies and time management;
- young teens tend to overcomplicate assignments and social situations; and
- dropping out of school results in low self-esteem and negative identities.

CHAPTER 4—AN EMOTIONAL COMMOTION

Emotions rule in the teenage brain, and the dictator is advocating anarchy. Neurotransmitters, hormones, and brain changes all work together for an emotional invasion of the teenage brain.

In this chapter, you learned that . . .

- teenagers are naturally drawn to wild and crazy things, which may include dangerous and harmful activities;
- they are controlled by the emotional part of the brain;
- they frequently misunderstand facial and body language;
- they often feel as though no one understands them;
- progesterone in girls lets stress run wild; and
- teenagers benefit from structure and guidance provided by adults.

CHAPTER 5—EMOTIONS GONE AWRY

At-risk students often lose control of their emotions and suffer consequences that haunt them for years. Learning to control aggression, recklessness, and depression takes direct instruction along with calm and clear role modeling.

In this chapter, you learned that . . .

- the amygdala in boys' brains are much more active than they are in adults' brains;
- testosterone agitates the amygdala, which leads boys to fight;
- violent video games increase hostility in boys;
- teenagers are more negative in spirit than adults are; and
- emotionally and behaviorially disturbed students have more dark thoughts and more trouble remembering things than do other teens.

CHAPTER 6—THE SOCIAL LIVES OF TEENS

Friendship, loyalty, and companionship are important factors in establishing identity and self-esteem. As at-risk teenagers mature, they rely on close friends for unconditional acceptance, wild fun, and rowdy whimsy.

In this chapter, you learned that . . .

- at-risk students often rely on peers because of a lack of parental support;
- teenagers learn to solve problems and negotiate by hanging and talking with one another;
- experimenting with various activities and friends is important in identity formation;
- dating and falling in love produce dopamine and make the teens feel great; and
- teens are not mentally or emotionally able to cope with breakups as easily as adults are, which may lead to their having depression or even committing suicide.

CHAPTER 7—GETTING PHYSICAL

Uncomfortable, misinformed, apprehensive—it must be puberty. During this time, teenagers commonly feel as though they don't fit in their own skin. Puberty is a time of great physical change, and teens benefit from emotional support and guidance from adults.

In this chapter, you learned that . . .

- puberty starts in the brain;
- the gay male brain has a smaller hypothalamus than does that of the straight male;
- eating disorders are primarily a cultural factor, though the brain also plays a role;
- sexuality is determined at birth;
- steroids activate the hypothalamus, resulting in anger and aggression;
- brain changes are the reason that teenagers have a difficult time waking up in the morning; and
- sleep-deprived adolescents are more likely to lose emotional control.

CHAPTER 8—MEETING SPECIAL CHALLENGES

The at-risk teen faces a variety of issues that make school challenging and frustrating. Neuroscientists are giving us an added glimpse into the disorders and activities that are prevalent in middle school and high school students.

In this chapter, you learned that . . .

- ADHD students have smaller brains, though this factor does not affect their intelligence;
- words can damage the brain just as physical and sexual abuse does;
- cutting gives a rush of pleasure; and
- adolescents living in poverty spend a great deal of time ensuring their own safety, making it difficult to focus on academics.

CHAPTER 9—ADDICTION: ALCOHOL, DRUGS, AND SMOKING

Addiction is a slippery slope. Once an adolescent starts down this path, life can quickly spiral out of control. The many changes going on in the adolescent brain make this a window of sensitivity for addiction.

In this chapter, you learned that . . .

- adolescents become addicted quickly;
- teenagers are resistant to treatment;
- teenagers do not get the same warning signals from their brains that adults do telling them that they have imbibed too much;
- teenagers lose inhibitions quickly, which lead to risk-taking behavior; and
- after binge drinking, teenagers can lose short-term memory capabilities for a month.

CHAPTER 10—ONE MORE CHANCE: EDUCATION IN JUVENILE CORRECTIONAL FACILITIES

Juvenile correctional facilities are the final chance to educate and prepare teenagers for the real world. The revolving-door nature of correctional programs makes it difficult for teachers to maintain consistency and continuity. Flexibility is their greatest strength. These teachers play an important and valuable role in helping those teens in the most desperate need.

In this chapter, you learned that . . .

- juveniles commit more impulsive crimes than planned crimes;
- the majority of adolescent homicide victims are their mothers' abusers;
- the U.S. Supreme Court compared the adolescent brain to one of a mentally retarded person's in its ability to make good decisions and thus decided to make executing teenagers illegal (we were the last industrialized country to come to this conclusion); and
- the prefrontal cortex is inactive in students with conduct disorder.

abstinence   Voluntary denial of sex of any kind.

acne   Bumps on the skin caused by hormone changes during puberty.

addiction   Repeated use of substances or behaviors that are harmful.

ADHD (attention deficit hyperactivity disorder)   A neurological disorder that involves hyperactivity, impulsivity, and an inability to focus.

adolescence   The transition between childhood and adulthood, from age 11 to 19.

amygdala   The part of the brain that processes and remembers emotions; it is involved in anger and fear.

anorexia nervosa   An eating disorder that involves self-starvation; anorexics turn away from food to control their lives.

at risk   Threat of dropping out of school.

attachment disorder   When normal attachment to parents does not occur within the first 2 years of life, which results in multiple social and emotional problems.

axon   The part of the neuron that sends information to other neurons.

basal ganglia   The part of the brain associated with motor control, thinking, and emotion.

binge drinking   Four alcoholic drinks for a woman and five for a man within a short period.

body image   Awareness and perception of one's body.

body language   Method of communicating through body movements and gestures.

brain   Part of the central nervous system located in the skull; the region responsible for storing, organizing, and retrieving information.

bulimia nervosa   An eating disorder that involves binging on food and then purging; bulimics turn to food to control their lives.

cerebellum   The part of the brain in control of physical movement.

chat room   A forum via computers for live conversation with others.

child abuse   Physical, sexual, and emotional assault and neglect.

cingulate system   Detects emotional meaning; part of the limbic system.

clique   A restricted social group.

cognition   The process of thinking.

cognitive neuroscience   The scientific study of the brain by neuroscientists, psychologists, and educationists.

corpus callosum   A network of neurons that connects the left and right hemispheres of the brain.

cortisol   Hormone released under stress; reduces the immune system and memory; increases blood pressure and heart rate.

crush   Short-lived feeling of affection for another person.

dendrite   Part of a neuron that receives messages from other neurons; one neuron may possess thousands of dendrites.

depression   A condition in which an individual is sad, lethargic, and unmotivated.

dopamine   A neurotransmitter in the brain that makes a person feel good.

EEG (electroencephalography)   Technology that measures electrical activity in the brain.

egocentrism   The inability to take someone else's perspective.

e-mail   Sending messages to others on a computer via modem or telephone lines.

endorphins   Peptides that give a sense of well-being and reduce pain.

epinephrine   A hormone; also known as adrenaline.

estrogen   A female hormone involved with menstruation, breast development, and pregnancy.

facebook   A social Internet site.

fMRI scans   Functional magnetic resonance imaging; brain-imaging technology that examines the functions of the brain.

frontal lobes   A part of the brain involved in decision making, language, problem solving, planning, and controlling.

gang   A group of individuals who share common characteristics and engage in criminal activity.

gay   Homosexual male (may also suggest lesbian).

glial   Brain cells that give support and protection to neurons.

heterosexual   Physical, romantic, and spiritual attraction between individuals of the opposite sex.

hippocampus   A part of the brain associated with transferring short-term memory into long-term memory.

HIV/AIDS (human immunodeficiency virus/acquired immune deficiency syndrome)   Disease that is transmitted through bodily fluids and attacks the immune system; there is no known cure.

homosexual   Physical, romantic, and spiritual attraction between individuals of the same sex.

hypothalamus   Part of the brain in control of pain, pleasure, hunger, thirst, and sexual desire.

identity   A person's physical, sexual, vocational, and spiritual makeup.

identity crisis   The act of searching for and discovering your identity.

Internet   Interconnected computers throughout the world.

juvenile   Not considered an adult by the law.

juvenile delinquent   A juvenile who violates the law.

leptin   A hormone that regulates appetite and metabolism.

lesbian   A homosexual female.

limbic system   A part of the brain involved in emotion and emotional memories.

LOL   *Laugh out loud* in Internet lingo.

melatonin   Nature's sleeping pill, released by the brain.

menstruation   The uterine wall of females sheds and bleeds approximately every 28 days; often referred to as a period.

MP3 player   Electronic device that stores and plays digital music; an iPod is similar technology.

music downloading   Copying a song or album from the Internet; iTunes is a popular music downloading website.

myelination   Insulates neurons so that they can communicate more efficiently.

neuron   A brain cell that consists of dendrites, an axon, and a cell body.

neuroscience   The study of the nervous system and the brain.

nocturnal emission   Seminal ejaculation during sleep; often referred to as a wet dream.

norepinephrine   A hormone that releases energy.

obesity   State of being overweight to the point of being unhealthy.

oxytocin   A hormone that also operates as a neurotransmitter, creating feelings of bonding and trust.

parietal lobes   A part of the brain associated with touch, temperature, and pain.

peer pressure   Influence by a group of people on another person's actions or thoughts.

PET scan   Positron emission tomography scan; a three-dimensional view of the brain that shows the structure and functions in the brain.

pruning   Elimination of synaptic connections and dendrites in the brain.

pseudostupidity   Tendency to apply overly complex solutions to simple problems.

puberty   The stage in life when an individual becomes capable of reproduction.

search engine   An Internet resource that allows users to find and retrieve information and documents; Google is a popular search engine.

self-esteem   A person's view of himself or herself, positive or negative.

serotonin   A neurotransmitter that acts as a calming agent.

STD (sexually transmitted disease)   A disease or infection that is contracted through sexual contact.

stress   Outside worries that affect the individual.

substance abuse   Overindulgence in a harmful substance, such as drugs or alcohol.

synaptic connection   A location of communication between two neurons.

temporal lobes   A part of the brain involved in hearing and memory.

testosterone   A male hormone required for sperm production and secondary sexual characteristics, such as pubic hair and a lower voice.

text messaging   Writing and receiving short messages online or on mobile phones.

URL (uniform resource locator)   The address of a site on the Internet.

YouTube   A free video-sharing website.

Bibliography

Adolescent smoking statistics. (2003). Retrieved April 25, 2007, from the American Lung Association website, www.lungusa.org/site/pp.asp?c=dvLUK 9O0E&b=39868

Aguilera, A., Selgas, R., Codoceo, R., & Bajo, A. (2000). Uremic anorexia: A consequence of persistently high brain serotonin levels? The tryptophan/serotonin disorder hypothesis. *Peritoneal Dialysis International, 20*(6), 810–816.

Allen, R. H. (2001). *Impact teaching: Ideas and strategies for teachers to maximize student learning.* Boston: Allyn & Bacon.

Allgeier, E. R., & Albert, R. (2000). *Sexual interactions.* New York: Houghton Mifflin.

Allman, J. (1999). *Evolving brains.* New York: Scientific American Library.

Amen, D. (1999). *Change your brain, change your life: The breakthrough program for conquering anxiety, depression, obsessiveness, anger, and impulsiveness.* San Diego, CA: Three Rivers Press.

Amen, D. G. (2002). *Healing ADD: The breakthrough program that allows you to see and heal the six types of attention deficit disorder.* New York: Putnam.

American Psychological Association. (2000). *Diagnostic and statistical manual of mental disorders* (4th ed., text revision). Washington, DC: American Psychological Association.

American Psychological Association. (2004, December 5). *Just like us: Chimpanzee brains are asymmetrical in key areas and their handedness reflects it.* Retrieved June 25, 2005, from www.apa.org/releases/chimpbrains.html

Ames, C. (1999). Motivation: What teachers need to know. In A. C. Ornstein & L. S. Behar Horenstein (Eds.), *Contemporary issues in curriculum* (2nd ed., pp. 135–144). Boston: Allyn & Bacon.

Arehart-Treichel, J. (2002). Evidence builds for prefrontal cortex abnormality in conduct disorder. *Psychiatric News, 37*(7), 24.

Armstrong, T. (1999). *Seven kinds of smart: Identifying and developing your multiple intelligences.* New York: Plume.

Armstrong, T. (2000). *Multiple intelligences in the classroom.* Alexandria, VA: Association for Supervision and Curriculum Development.

Atwell, N. (1990). *In the middle: Writing, reading, and learning with adolescents.* Portsmouth, NH: Heinemann.

Bailey, B. A. (2000). *Easy to love, difficult to discipline.* New York: Perennial Currents.

Bailey, B. A. (2001). *Conscious discipline: Seven basic skills for brain smart classroom management.* Oviedo, FL: Loving Guidance.

Baird, A. A., Gruber, S. A., Fein, D. A., Maas, L. C., Steingard, R. J., Renshaw, P. F., et al. (1999). Functional magnetic resonance imaging of facial affect recognition in children and adolescents. *Journal of the American Academy of Child and Adolescent Psychiatry, 38*(2), 195–199.

Barbarich, N. (2002). Is there a common mechanism of serotonin dysregulation in anorexia nervosa and obsessive compulsive disorder? *Eating and Weight Disorders, 7*(3), 221–231.

Barry, L. M., & Messer, J. J. (2003). A practical application of self-management for students diagnosed with attention-deficit/hyperactivity disorder [Electronic version]. *Journal of Positive Behavior Interventions, 5*(4), 238–248. Retrieved January 17, 2005, from EBSCOhost Academic Search Premier Database.

Bartels, A., & Zeki, S. (2000). The neural basis of romantic love. *Neuroreport, 11*(17), 3828–3834.

Baverstock, A. C., & Finlay, F. (2003). Who manages the care of students with attention deficit hyperactivity disorder (ADHD) in higher education? [Electronic version]. *Child: Care, Health, and Development, 29*(3), 163–166. Retrieved January 17, 2005, from EBSCOhost Academic Search Premier Database.

Beck, A. T., Rush, A. J., Shaw, B. F., & Emery, G. (1979). *Cognitive therapy of depression.* New York: Guilford Press.

Bloom, F. E., Beal, M. F., & Kupfer, D. J. (2003). *The Dana guide to brain health.* New York: Free Press.

Borba, M. (2002). *Building moral intelligence: The seven essential virtues that teach kids to do the right thing.* San Francisco: Jossey-Bass.

Bremner, J. D. (2005). *Does stress damage the brain? Understanding trauma-related disorders from a neurological perspective.* New York: Norton.

Brendtro, L., Brokenleg, M., & VanBockern, S. (2002). *Reclaiming youth at risk*. Bloomington, IN: National Educational Service.

Brendtro, L., & du Toit, L. (2005). *RAP: Response ability pathways*. Cape Town, South Africa: Pretext.

Brendtro, L., & Shahbazian, M. (2004). *Troubled children and youth: Turning problems into opportunity*. Champaign, IL: Research Press.

Brooks, R. (1994). Children at risk: Fostering resilience and hope. *American Journal of Orthopsychiatry, 64*, 266–278.

Byrnes, J. P. (2001). *Minds, brains, and learning: Understanding the psychological and educational relevance of neuroscientific research*. New York: Guilford Press.

Caine, G., & Caine, R. (2001). *The brain, education, and the competitive edge*. Lanham, MD: Rowman & Littlefield Education.

Caine, R., Caine, G., McClinitic, C., & Klimek, K. (2005). *The 12 brain mind learning principles in action: The field book to "Making Connections: Teaching and the Human Brain."* Thousand Oaks, CA: Corwin Press.

Carbone, E. (2001). Arranging the classroom with an eye (and ear) to students with ADHD [Electronic version]. *Teaching Exceptional Children, 34*(2), 72–81. Retrieved October 17, 2004, from EBSCOhost Academic Search Premier Database.

Cardinal, R. N., & Everitt, B. J. (2004). Neural and psychological mechanisms underlying appetitive learning: Links to drug addiction. *Current Opinion in Neurobiology, 14*, 156–162.

Carskadon, M. (Ed.). (2002). *Adolescent sleep patterns: Biological, social, and psychological influences*. New York: Cambridge University Press.

Caulfield, J., Kidd, S., & Kocher, T. (2000). Brain-based instruction in action. *Educational Leadership, 58*(3), 62–65.

Chambers, R. A., Taylor, J. R., & Potenza, M. N. (2003, June). Developmental neurocircuitry of motivation in adolescence: A critical period of addiction vulnerability. *American Journal of Psychiatry, 160*(6), 1041–1052.

Christensen, D. (2003, September). Time to rethink the high school experience. *NCSA Today*. (Reprinted from *Scientific foundations of cognitive theory and therapy of depression*, by D. A. Clark, A. T. Beck, & B. Alford, 1999, New York: Wiley.)

Clarke, H. F., Dalley, J. W., Crofts, H. S., Robbins, T. W., & Roberts, A. C. (2004). Cognitive inflexibility after prefrontal serotonin depletion. *Science, 304*(5672), 878–880.

Cummins, J. (1986). Empowering minority students: A framework for intervention. *Harvard Educational Review, 56*, 18–36.

Damasio, A. R. (1994). *Descartes' error: Emotion, reason, and the human brain*. New York: Avon Books.

Damasio, A. R. (1999). *The feeling of what happens: Body and emotion in the making of consciousness*. New York: Harcourt.

Damasio, A. R. (2003). *Looking for Spinoza: Joy, sorrow, and the feeling brain*. New York: Harcourt.

D'Arcangelo, M. (2000a). How does the brain develop? A conversation with Steven Peterson. *Educational Leadership, 58*(3), 68–71.

D'Arcangelo, M. (2000b). The scientist in the crib: A conversation with Andrew Meltzoff. *Educational Leadership, 58*(3), 8–13.

Deci, E., Vallerand, E. R., Pelletier, L. G., & Ryan, R. M. (1991). Motivation and education: The self-determination perspective. *Educational Psychologist, 26*(3–4), 325–346.

Delfos, M. F. (2004). *Children and behavioural problems: Anxiety, aggression, depression, and ADHD—A biopsychological model with guidelines for diagnostics and treatment*. London: Kingsley.

Delisio, E. R. (2006). *Pairing at-risk high school, elementary kids benefits both*. Retrieved April 25, 2007, from the Education World website, www.education-world.com/a_admin/admin/admin456.shtml

Diamond, M. (1967). Extensive cortical depth measurements and neuron size increases in the cortex of environmentally enriched rats. *Journal of Comparative Neurology, 131*, 357–364.

Diamond, M. (1988). *Enriching heredity: The impact of the environment on the anatomy of the brain*. New York: Free Press.

Erlauer, L. (2003). *The brain-compatible classroom: Using what we know about learning to improve teaching*. Alexandria, VA: Association for Supervision and Curriculum Development.

Fairburn, C. G., & Harrison, P. J. (2003). Eating disorders. *The Lancet, 361*, 407–416.

Feingold, A. (1996). Cognitive gender differences: Where are they and why are they there? *Learning and Individual Differences, 8*, 25–32.

Feinstein, S. (2003). A case for middle school after-school programs in rural America. *Middle School Journal, 32*(3), 32–37.

Feinstein, S. (2004). *Secrets of the teenage brain: Research-based strategies for reaching and teaching today's adolescents*. San Diego, CA: The Brain Store.

Feinstein, S. (2007). *Parenting the teenage brain: Understanding a work in progress*. Lanham, MD: Rowman & Littlefield Education.

Feinstein, S. (Ed.). (2006). *The Praeger handbook of learning and the brain*. Westport, CT: Praeger.

Fisher, H. E., Aron, A., Mashek, D., Li, H., & Brown, L. L. (2002, October). Defining the brain systems of lust, romantic attraction, and attachment. *Archives of Sexual Behavior, 31*(5), 413–419.

Fisher, S. F. (n.d.). *Neurofeedback: A treatment for reactive attachment disorder.* Retrieved April 25, 2007, from www.eegspectrum.com/Articles/Articles/InHouseArticles/RAD/

Freeman, H. D., Cantalupo, C., & Hopkins, W. D. (2004). Asymmetries in the hippocampus and amygdala of chimpanzees (Pan troglodytes). *Behavioral Neuroscience, 118*(6), 1460–1465.

Futris, T. G., & McDowell, U. (2002). *Adolescents at risk: Sexual activity* [Family Life Month Packet at Ohio State University]. Retrieved April 25, 2007, from http://ohioline.osu.edu/flm02/pdf/FS13.pdf

Gardner, A. (2004). Fast food linked to obesity, insulin problems. *Health-DayNews.* Retrieved October 25, 2005, from www.healthfinder.gov/news/newsstory.asp?docID=523168

Gardner, H. (2000). *Intelligence reframed: Multiple intelligences for the 21st century.* New York: Basic Books.

Garrick-Duhaney, L. M. (2003). A practical approach to managing the behaviors of students with ADD [Electronic version]. *Intervention in School and Clinic, 38*(5), 267–279. Retrieved January 17, 2005, from EBSCOhost Academic Search Premier Database.

Gazzaniga, M. S., Ivry, R. B., & Mangun, G. R. (1998). *Cognitive neuroscience: Biology of the mind.* New York: Norton.

Gee, J. P. (2003). *What video games have to teach us about learning and literacy.* New York: Palgrave Macmillan.

Giedd, J., Blumenthal, J., Jeffries, N., Rajapakse, J., Vaituzis, C., Liu, H., et al. (1999). Development of the human corpus callosum during childhood and adolescence: A longitudinal MRI study. *Progress in Neuro-Psychopharmacology and Biological Psychiatry, 23*(4), 571–588.

Gillies, R., & Ashman, A. (1998). Behavior and interactions of children in cooperative groups in lower and middle elementary grades. *Journal of Educational Psychology, 90*(4), 746–757.

Goldberg, E. (2002). *The executive brain: Frontal lobes and the civilized mind.* New York: Oxford University Press.

Goleman, D. (2002). *Primal leadership: Realizing the power of emotional intelligence.* Boston: Harvard Business School.

Graham-Rowe, D. (2002). Teen angst rooted in busy brain. *New Scientist, 176*(2365), 16.

Greene, R. (2001). *The explosive child: A new approach for understanding and parenting easily frustrated, chronically inflexible children*. New York: HarperCollins.

Gunn, A. M., Richburg, R. W., & Smilkstein, R. (2006). *Igniting student potential: Teaching with the brain's natural learning process*. Thousand Oaks, CA: Corwin Press.

Hart, L. A. (1999). *Human brain and human learning*. Covington, WA: Books for Educators.

Heffner, M., & Eifert, G. H. (2004). *The anorexia workbook: How to accept yourself, heal suffering, and reclaim your life*. Oakland, CA: New Harbinger.

Helmuth, L. (2001). Addiction: Beyond the pleasure principle. *Science, 294*, 983–984.

Hughes, D. (2003). *Behavioral neurogenetics: A complementary strategy to understanding neuropsychiatric disorders*. Retrieved June 24, 2005, from http://neuropsychiatryreviews.com/apr03/npr_apr03_neurogenetics.html

Jacobs, B., Schall, M., & Scheibel, A. B. (1993). A quantitative dendritic analysis of Wernieke's area in humans. II. Gender, hemispheric, and environmental factors. *Journal of Comparative Neurology, 327*, 97–111.

Jensen, E. (2000). Learning smarter: The new science of teaching and training. San Diego, CA: The Brain Store.

Jensen, E. (2003). *Tools for engagement: Managing emotional states for learner success*. San Diego, CA: The Brain Store.

Jensen, E. (2005). *Teaching with the brain in mind* (2nd ed.). Alexandria, VA: Association for Supervision and Curriculum Development.

Johnson, S. (2004). Antonio Damasio's theory of thinking faster and faster. *Discover, 25*(5), 44–49.

Katchadourian, H. A. (1990). *The biological aspects of human sexuality*. Austin, TX: Holt, Rinehart, and Winston.

Kaufeldt, M. (1999). *Begin with the brain: Orchestrating the learner-centered classroom*. San Diego, CA: The Brain Store.

Kim, J., & Diamond, D. (2002). The stressed hippocampus, synaptic plasticity, and lost memories. *Nature Reviews Neuroscience, 3*(6), 453–462.

Kovalik, S. J., & Olsen, K. D. (2002). *Exceeding expectations: A user's guide to implementing brain research in the classroom* (2nd ed.). Covington, WA: Books for Educators.

Laumann, E. O., Gagnon, J. H., Michael, R. T., & Michaels, S. (2000). *The social organization of sexuality: Sexual practices in the United States*. Chicago: The University of Chicago Press.

Lazaer, D. (2004). *Higher-order thinking the multiple intelligences way.* Chicago: Zephyr Press.

LeDoux, J. (1996). *The emotional brain: The mysterious underpinnings of emotional life.* New York: Simon and Schuster.

LeDoux, J. (2002). *Synaptic self.* Toronto, Ontario, Canada: Viking Penguin Books.

Lerner, R., & Benson, P. (Eds.). (2003). *Developmental assets and asset-building communities: Implications for research, policy, and practice.* Minneapolis, MN: Search Institute.

Lupien, S. J., & Lepage, M. (2001). Stress, memory, and the hippocampus: Can't live with it, can't live without it. *Behavioural Brain Research, 127*(1–2), 137–158.

Lurie, K. (2005). *ADHD brain scan.* Retrieved June 25, 2005, from www .sciencentral.com/articles/view.php3?language=english&type=&article _id=218392460

MacDonald, A. (2003). Imaging studies bring ADHD into sharper focus. *Brainwork: The Neuroscience Newsletter, 13*(2). Retrieved June 25, 2005, from www.dana.org/pdf/periodicals/brainwork_0403.pdf

Marzano, R. J. (2001). *Designing a new taxonomy of educational objectives.* Thousand Oaks, CA: Corwin Press.

Marzano, R. J. (2003). *Classroom management that works: Research-based strategies for development.* Alexandra, VA: Association for Supervision and Curriculum Development.

Marzano, R. J., Pickering, D. J., & Pollock, J. E. (2001). *Classroom instruction that works.* Alexandra, VA: Association for Supervision and Curriculum Development.

Mayer, J. D., Salovey, P., Caruso, D. R., & Sigarenios, G. (2001). Emotional intelligence as a standard intelligence. *Emotion, 1*, 232–242.

Mendez-Sanchez, N., Ponciano-Rodrigoez, G., Chavez-Tapia, N., & Uribe, M. (2005). Effects of leptin on biliary lipids: Potential consequences for gallstone formation and therapy in obesity. *Current Drug Targets: Immune, Endocrine, and Metabolic Disorders, 5*(2), 203–208.

National Dropout Prevention Center. (2007). [Website]. Retrieved March 7, 2007, from www.dropoutprevention.org

Nestler, E. J., & Malenka, R. C. (2004). The addicted brain. *Scientific American, 290*(3), 78–85.

Niehoff, D. (1999). *The biology of violence: How understanding the brain, behavior, and environment can break the vicious circle of aggression.* New York: Free Press.

NPR. (2007). *Sex education in America: An NPR/Kaiser/Kennedy School poll.* Retrieved April 26, 2007, from www.npr.org/templates/story/story.php ?storyId=1622610

Ortiz, A. (2003, Spring). Adolescent brain development and legal culpability. *Juvenile Justice Center* (Criminal Justice section). Retrieved April 25, 2007, from the American Bar Association website, www.abanet.org/crimjust/ juvjus/Adolescence.pdf

PBS. (2002) *Frontline: Interviews inside the teenage brain.* Retrieved July 6, 2005, from www.pbs.org/wgbh/pages/frontline/shows/teenbrain/

Phelps, E., O'Connor, K. J., Cunningham, W. A., Funayama, E. S., Sumie, E., Gatenby, J. C., et al. (2002). Performance on indirect measures of race evaluation predicts amygdala activation. In J. Cacioppo et al. (Eds.), *Foundations of social neuroscience* (pp. 615–627). Cambridge, MA: MIT Press.

Phillips, P. E. M., Stuber, G. D., Heien, M. L. A. V., Wightman, R. M., & Carell, R. M. (2003). Subsecond dopamine release promotes cocaine seeking. *Nature, 422,* 614–618.

Pipher, M. (1994). *Reviving Ophelia: Saving the selves of adolescent girls.* New York: Putnam.

Popham, J. (2001). *The truth about testing: An educator's call to action.* Alexandria, VA: Association for Supervision and Curriculum Development.

Popham, J. (2002). *Classroom assessment: What teachers need to know* (3rd ed.). Boston: Allyn & Bacon.

Preston, S. D., & deWaal, F. B. M. (2002). Empathy: Its ultimate and proximate bases. *Behavioral and Brain Sciences, 25*(1), 1–71.

Restak, R. (1995). *Brainscapes.* New York: Hyperion.

Restak, R. (2003). *The new brain.* New York: Rodale.

Rice, P., & Dolgin, K. G. (2004). *The adolescent: Development, relationships, and culture* (11th ed.). Needham Heights, MA: Allyn & Bacon.

Ronis, D. (2000). *Brain-compatible assessments.* Glenview, IL: Skylight Professional Development.

Rothenberg, J., McDermott, P., & Martin, G. (1998). Changes in pedagogy: A qualitative result of teaching heterogeneous classes. *Teaching and Teacher Education, 14*(6), 633–642.

Rothschild, B. (2000). *The body remembers: The psychophysiology of trauma and trauma treatment.* New York: Norton.

Salend, S. J., Elhoweris, H., & Van Garderen, D. (2003). Educational interventions for students with ADD [Electronic version]. *Intervention in School and Clinic, 38*(5), 280–285. Retrieved January 17, 2005, from EBSCOhost Academic Search Premier Database.

Santrock, J. W. (2005). *Adolescence* (10th ed.). Boston: McGraw-Hill.

Science a GoGo. (2001). *Stress and aggression reinforce each other*. Retrieved July 2, 2005, from www.scienceagogo.com/news/20040903231503data_trunc _sys.shtml

Sexuality Information and Education Council of the United States. (2004). *Guidelines for comprehensive sexuality education: Kindergarten through 12th grade* (3rd ed.). Retrieved July 2, 2005, from www.siecus.org/pubs/ guidelines/guidelines.pdf

Slavkin, M. (2002). Brain science in the classroom. *Principal Leadership, 2*(8), 21–23.

Smilkstein, R. (2003). *We're born to learn: Using the brain's natural learning process to create today's curriculum*. Thousand Oaks, CA: Corwin Press.

Sousa, D. (2001). *How the brain learns* (2nd ed.). Thousand Oaks, CA: Corwin Press.

Sousa, D. (2004). *How the brain learns to read*. Thousand Oaks, CA: Corwin Press.

Stengle, J. (2004, December 4). *Obesity is rising sharply among U.S. preschoolers* [Associated Press article].

Stiggins, R. (2002). Assessment crisis: The absence of assessment for learning. *Phi Delta Kappan, 83*(10), 758–765.

Stilwell, B., Galvin, M., Kopta, S. M., & Kopta, S. (2000). *Right vs. wrong: Raising a child with a conscience*. Bloomington: Indiana University Press.

Strauch, B. (2004). *The primal teen: What the new discoveries about the teenage brain tell us about our kids*. New York: Bantam Doubleday.

Sylwester, R. (1995). *A celebration of neurons*. Alexandria, VA: Association for Supervision and Curriculum Development.

Teens With Problems. (2007). *Oppositional defiant disorder (ODD) versus conduct disorder*. Retrieved April 26, 2007, from http://teenswithproblems .com/conduct_disorder.html

Thompson, J. G. (1998). *Discipline survival kit for the secondary teacher*. San Francisco: Jossey-Bass.

Tileston, D. W. (2000). *What every teacher should know about motivation*. Thousand Oaks, CA: Corwin Press.

Tobin, M., Nelson, J., & Castellanos, F. (1999). Development of the human corpus callosum during childhood and adolescence: A longitudinal MRI study. *Progress in Neuro-Psychopharmacology and Biological Psychiatry, 23*, 557–588.

Tomlinson, C. (1996). *Differentiating instruction in mixed ability classrooms*. Alexandria, VA: Association for Supervision and Curriculum Development.

Tompkins, G. (2005). *Literacy for the 21st century: A balanced approach*. Upper Saddle River, NJ: Prentice Hall.

Toye, S. (2001). *Study shows obesity bad for the mind, too*. Retrieved June 24, 2005, from www.sciencedaily.com/releases/2001/05/010529071515.htm

U.S. Office of Special Education Programs. (2003). *Identifying and treating attention deficit hyperactivity disorder: A resource for school and home*. Retrieved June 24, 2005, from www.ed.gov/teachers/needs/speced/adhd/adhd -resource-pt1.doc

Wagner, U., Gais, S., Haider, H., Verleger, R., & Born, J. (2004). Sleep inspires insight. *Nature, 427*(6972), 352–355.

Walsh, D. (2004). *Why do they act that way? A survival guide to the adolescent brain for you and your teen*. New York: Free Press.

Walsh, P. (2000). A hands-on approach to understanding the brain. *Educational Leadership, 58*(3), 76–78.

Wang, G. J., Volkow, N. D., Logan, J., Pappas, N. R., Wong, C. T., Zhu, W., et al. (2001). Brain dopamine and obesity. *Lancet, 357*(9253), 354–357.

Wilkinson, I., & Fung, I. (2002). Small-group composition and peer effects. *International Journal of Educational Research, 37*(5), 483–504.

Wolfe, P. (2001). *Brain matters: Translating research into classroom practice*. Alexandria, VA: Association for Supervision and Curriculum Development.

YMCA of the USA. (2001). *After school for America's teens: A national survey of teen attitudes and behaviors in the hours after school*. An executive summary report by the YMCA of the USA. Retrieved March 26, 2004, from the Drug Policy Alliance website, www.drugpolicy.org/library/bibliography/ afterschool

Young, J. E., Beck, A. T., & Weinberger, A. (1993). Depression. In D. H. Barlow (Ed.), *Clinical handbook of psychological disorders: A step-by-step treatment manual* (2nd ed., pp. 240–277). New York: Guilford Press.

Yurgelun-Todd, D. A., Killgore, W. D., & Young, A. D. (2002). Sex differences in cerebral tissue volume and cognitive performance during adolescence. *Psychological Reports, 91*(3, Pt. 1), 743–757.

Zhou, J. N., Hofman, M. A., Gooren, L. J., & Swaab, D. F. (1995). A sex difference in the human brain and its relation to transsexuality. *Nature, 378*, 68–70.

Zull, J. E. (2002). *The art of changing the brain: Enriching teaching by exploring the biology of learning*. Herndon, VA: Stylus.

Index

abstract thinking, 6, 39
accountability, 18, 24
adrenaline, 47, 53, 132
aggression, 59–63, 66–67, 91, 105,
    118, 127–28
altruism, 54
amygdala, 8, 31–32, 52, 56–57, 60,
    63–64, 69, 100, 104, 119, 127, 131
analytical reasoning/thinking, 50
anger, 8, 19, 45, 52, 57, 61, 66, 91,
    119–21, 128, 131
anxiety, 40, 47, 62, 67, 70, 103, 105,
    117, 121
assessment/testing, 25–26, 29, 30,
    47, 50, 56, 105, 117
auditory, 56
axon, 4, 131

basal ganglia, 67, 97, 131
Bloom's taxonomy, 25, 28–29
body: image, 84, 89–90, 131;
    language, 63, 127, 131
boys, 60, 63–64, 73, 76–77, 84, 86,
    91, 102, 118, 127
brain cells, 4, 131
Broca's area, 28, 31
bullying, 2, 61–63, 66, 119

cerebral hemispheres (right and left),
    28, 31, 99–100, 131
cingulate gyrus, 67–68, 132
classroom environment, 126
cooperative learning, 24
coping skills, 2, 48, 57, 64, 81,
    102–3, 106, 115, 121
corpus callosum, 31, 99, 132
cortex: cerebral, 56; prefrontal, 57,
    67, 69, 77, 100, 118–19, 130
cortisol, 47, 69, 132

decision-making skills, 7, 45–46,
    49–50, 57–58, 80, 86, 104, 109,
    114, 118, 132
dendrite, 1, 3–5, 105, 132
*Diagnostic and Statistical Manual of
    Mental Disorders*, 118
differentiated instruction, 23
direct instruction, 37, 46, 57, 116,
    126–27, 148
dopamine, 19, 54, 59, 65, 75, 80, 89,
    105, 108, 110, 128, 132

empathy, 33, 54, 57, 64, 119
endorphin, 19, 102, 132
enrichment, 4, 105, 146

estrogen, 53–54, 80, 84, 132
exercise, 48–49, 64, 92, 120
expectations, 38, 41, 60, 65, 68, 89, 96, 120
extrinsic motivation, 121

fear, 31, 40, 56, 105, 131
feedback, 26, 60, 101, 121
fMRI, 3, 4, 31, 80, 99, 100, 132

gangs, 48–49, 57, 61, 86, 119, 133
gender. *See* boys; girls
girls, 43, 45, 47, 53–55, 60, 69, 73–74, 80–81, 84–86, 91, 102–3, 109, 127
goals, 26, 43, 57–58, 68, 98, 106
graphic organizer, 24

high school, 2, 4–7, 9, 11, 15, 21–22, 35–36, 40–43, 45–46, 50, 51, 54, 59, 66–67, 73, 77, 81, 85–87, 91, 93, 96, 129
hippocampus, 31, 69, 74, 108–9, 133
hormone, 3, 45, 47, 60, 69, 88, 91, 127, 131–34
hypothalamus, 84, 87–88, 91, 128, 133

identity, 9, 10, 41, 52, 77, 9, 85, 88, 127–28, 133
immune system, 47, 132–33
impulse control, 1, 52, 60, 64, 91, 106
independent study, 25
Internet, 25, 76, 97, 132–34
intrinsic motivation, 120

journaling, 21, 24, 26, 30, 48, 92

language, 8, 15, 28, 31–32, 116
learning style, 25, 28, 60

lecture, 15, 24, 37, 54, 111
left cerebral hemisphere. *See* cerebral hemispheres (right and left)
leptin, 89, 133
limbic system, 99, 132–33
long-term memory, 31, 74, 133

mastery, 25
mentor, 24, 42, 55, 86, 117
metaphors, 27
middle school, 7, 10–11, 17, 21–22, 35–40, 43, 49–50, 59, 61–62, 65, 78, 81, 83, 93, 103–4, 109, 129
multiple intelligences, 15, 22–23, 28, 68, 126
myelin (myelination), 3, 6–8, 49, 133
myelination. *See* myelin (myelination)

neuron, 3, 4–6, 25, 28, 69, 131–34
neurotransmitters, 19, 60, 69, 89, 108, 127, 132, 134
nicotine, 110, 199
No Child Left Behind Act, 24
novelty, 19, 59, 75, 115, 126

oppositional behavior, 67–68, 114, 117–18

parent, 2, 4, 8–11, 20, 32, 36, 48, 50–53, 55–56, 62, 64–65, 68, 74, 78, 85, 87, 92–93, 96–104, 108, 110, 113, 128, 131
parietal lobes, 5, 134
peers, 2, 8, 13, 18, 22, 24–25, 43, 48, 56–59, 62, 65, 67, 72–75, 77–79, 85, 97, 99, 101, 104, 108, 110–11, 120, 128, 134
PET scan, 3, 100, 134

poverty, 13, 16, 41, 95, 105–6, 129
praise, 36, 60, 64
problem-solving, 6–7, 22, 25, 27,
    56–58, 73, 79, 93, 104, 106, 118,
    120, 126, 132
progesterone, 47, 69, 127
pruning, 3, 5–6, 8, 49, 134
puberty, 3, 8–10, 45, 47, 54, 60, 69,
    80, 83–85, 88, 128, 131, 134

reinforcement, 121
right cerebral hemisphere. *See* cerebral
    hemispheres (right and left)
role-model, 48, 57, 61, 68, 103, 127
role-play, 20, 23, 27, 58, 68

self-esteem, 41, 68, 70, 76–77, 79,
    84–86, 90, 105–6, 111, 126–27,
    134

self-regulation, 60
serotonin, 54, 60, 65, 69, 89, 102,
    105, 119, 134
short-term memory, 5, 31, 64,
    107–9, 129
stress, 24, 26, 32, 35, 39–40, 45–49,
    57, 69, 74, 92, 95, 99, 102–5,
    108, 110, 116–17, 120–21, 127,
    132, 134
study skills, 7, 35, 98
synapse, 4

temporal lobe, 5, 67, 134
testosterone, 59–60, 64, 80, 84, 91,
    127, 134

visual/spatial, 56, 117

Wernicke's area, 28–29

About the Author

Sheryl Feinstein, EdD, is associate professor at Augustana College in Sioux Falls, South Dakota. She is the author of the book *Secrets of the Teenage Brain* (2004) and the editor and coauthor of *The Praeger Handbook of Learning and the Brain* (2006) and *Parenting the Teenage Brain: Understanding a Work in Progress* (2007). During the summer of 2006, she was a fellow at Oxford's Harris Manchester College and conducted research in the area of cognitive neuroscience with the adolescent. She was awarded a lecture/researcher Fulbright Scholarship to Tanzania for the 2007–2008 school year.

In addition to teaching at Augustana College, she consults at a correctional facility for adolescent boys and at a separate site for emotionally and behaviorally disturbed adolescents in Minnesota. The correctional facility has received state and local recognition for their exemplary practices and service.

Before being at Augustana College, Feinstein taught in public schools and was a curriculum consultant for a K–12 school district in Minnesota. She also started an alternative school for high school students and was a regional liaison in Minnesota to facilitate integrating national and state standards into alternative programs. She presents nationally and internationally on the adolescent brain. She can be contacted by e-mail at sheryl.feinstein@augie.edu.